Marlborough
Man

RESTRICTED
AREA
ELECTRONIC
SURVEILLANCE
EQUIPMENT IN
OPERATION
Visitors must
report to office
on arrival

Marlborough Man

{ *A quintessentially Kiwi story of an accidental wine-industry trailblazer* }

ALLAN SCOTT, MNZM

with

Eric Arnold

Additional research and interviews
by Tessa Nicholson

HarperCollins*Publishers*

To my family, who have always been so supportive,
and to all my fellow workers, without whom none
of this would have been possible

CONTENTS

FOREWORD

To gain a fair reflection of vintage conditions each year, I have a trusted voice in each region. I need a 'straight-shooter' who will provide a true account of weather conditions and crop quality. Allan Scott is my contact in Marlborough, New Zealand's largest and most important wine region.

He is also my 'go-to' man when I want to know which vineyards suffered frost damage, how Marlborough's wineries survived an earthquake or what is the region's current potential for further vineyard expansion. His always-forthright comments may get him into trouble occasionally, as you will read in these pages, but they are exactly what I need when researching a story. Marlborough's business is Allan's business; for me, and countless others, Allan *is* the Marlborough Man.

This is a fascinating and very candid record of one man's intrepid journey from farm worker to winery owner. It should be compulsory reading for anyone who is captured by the romance of wine and tempted to plant a vineyard. To achieve the sort of success enjoyed by Allan and his family requires great determination to surmount every obstacle; expertise in every aspect of winemaking, from growing plants to closing a sale; and more than a little luck.

Our paths intersected for the first time in the early 1970s, when we both worked for Montana Wines, although I was stuck in an Auckland office while Allan worked in the more glamorous, if dustier, setting of a Marlborough vineyard. Until I read Allan's account of the development of vineyards in Marlborough I'd forgotten what a crazy, precarious and yet wildly brilliant project this was. I attended the official opening at the Brancott vineyard. Few of the dignitaries present would have guessed that such an ambitious development at times hung by a rather frayed thread. The efforts of Allan's 'unsung heroes' may just have made the difference between success and failure for the most important event in the history of this country's wine industry.

As well as being an important snapshot of a critical time in the development of the New Zealand wine industry and a chronicle of one family's part in it, *Marlborough Man* is an amusing and engaging read. Allan's digressions cover topics as diverse as misadventures with cats, his tendency to fall asleep at the dinner table, how he and Daniel Le Brun escaped being snowbound in the French Alps, and the perils of owning an exotic sports car. He's a natural storyteller, with an eye for detail and an ability to see the humorous side of most situations.

This at times very personal book reveals much about Allan and the strong bonds within his family. His children play an increasingly important role in running the Allan Scott winery as the story progresses. Their combined enthusiasm and capacity for hard work are now the fuel that drives a business that started with just Allan and Cathy at the helm. And so the adventure continues, leaving the Marlborough Man time to ponder a job well done, while keeping a crafty eye on future opportunities.

Bob Campbell, MW

INTRODUCTION

MARLBOROUGH MAN ... I ADMIT, THE TITLE IS a bit of a joke. It's one that no wine drinkers are in on, yet seemingly everyone in New Zealand's wine industry loves to tell. Several Kiwis who have made their living — or their fortunes — from fermented grape juice are all too happy to portray themselves as the Marlborough Man, *the* pioneer of this region. If it will mean the sale of an extra bottle at the cellar door or an extra case to a restaurant or a supermarket, just about any winery will claim it was the first to drive a stake into the dry Marlborough dirt. Or the first to grow grapes. Or the first to make and sell a Sauvignon Blanc in a bottle rather than as a component of a medium cask white.

True, New Zealand's wine industry dates back more than a century, rather than a mere few decades. But you needn't crack open more than one history book to learn that no one in New Zealand actually made good-tasting wine until about the late 1970s or even the early 1980s. Even to call what we made before then 'swill' might be a little on the generous side. The lion's share of New Zealand's wine history might be best summed up by old photographs

17

from the 1920s and 1930s, showing the truck from which Corbans sold wine at fairs and A&P shows. The signage on the vehicle makes it look as though Corbans were selling snake oil. (Given the choice between that and anything made of New Zealand-grown and -fermented grapes up to 1980 or so, I would actually take the snake oil.) No matter how many experienced or trained viticulturists visited or worked in New Zealand — the most famous being Romeo Bragato in 1895 — no single person managed to produce a drop of palatable wine until after 'ground zero' was identified and planted. That place was the Brancott Valley in Marlborough — specifically, the spot where today we celebrate the Marlborough Wine Festival each year – and the year was 1973.

Even so, things still took several more years to come together. While plenty of people claim some measure of responsibility for selecting or purchasing or planting the land, there were many of us working with grapes, wine, or both, in Marlborough in the early 1970s. We were all working together in a new industry that offered more question-marks than promises, but for the time being allowed many of us simply to put food on the table. Today, if you drive the length of the Wairau Valley from Blenheim towards Renwick, you will see thousands of perfectly planted, beautiful rows of Sauvignon Blanc. Parallel, pristine green lines stretch from north to south, as if there had been a master plan of sorts for Marlborough, right from the beginning. But nothing could be further from the truth.

On the arid, windy, winter mornings in 1973, when planting commenced at Marlborough's first large-scale vineyard, Brancott, I was tearing down fences, planting vine cuttings and driving posts into the hard, unforgiving dirt right alongside many who would later become the most recognisable names in New Zealand wine. To my left and right were people who would go on to make some of the greatest contributions to the industry, yet receive barely a mention in the history books. Others would be forgotten entirely. But all of us who gathered each morning below the imposing hills to the west and south as we awaited the day's instructions, the dust stinging our

ABOVE: Handpicking on the Montana vineyard, 1975
FACING PAGE: At the Allan Scott Family Winery today

eyes, had one very important thing in common. Along with our eagerness to do a day's work and earn a dollar, we were completely and utterly *clueless*. The blind were leading the blind.

Kiwis from north and south, native Marlburians, farmers, foremen, managers, fathers, mothers — none of us had any idea how to plant a vineyard, large or small, how to train vines, how to grow a healthy crop of grapes, how to make palatable wine. Not even the managers dispatched from Auckland's and Gisborne's established vineyards knew much beyond left and right. Marlborough's Brancott vineyard was the first 400 hectares of the Montana Wine Company's 1,173-hectare, $1.3-million gamble.* (Today, the same amount of planted Marlborough land would cost well over $100 million.) And we were the misfits who, collectively, could have just as easily ensured the bet was a washout rather than one that paid off as handsomely as it did — and ultimately resulted in a product now beloved the world over.

---

* Unless otherwise noted, all dollar amounts in this book are New Zealand dollars.

A family lunch at the vineyard: left to right, George, Josh, Jemima, Cathy, Oliver, me, Gus (partly obscured), Victoria and Sara

This is all to say that there was no original Marlborough man in grapes, wine, or both. Among those of us who consider ourselves pioneers or advancers of New Zealand wine, some were more dedicated than others. Some were more talented. But all of us were extremely lucky to be in the right place at the right time. Over the next several years, we learned from each other through trial, through error, and through outright farce. We are still doing our best at all three …

I have never claimed to be the first in Marlborough wine, nor have I ever claimed to be the best. Like every other family agricultural business, we have had our challenges, successes, failures and near-misses. More than I can even recall to fill these pages. What we have done, however, is survived and endured as a family, as a business and as a family business — one we are intensely proud of, not just as farmers or winemakers, but as New Zealanders.

It is my hope that you will not read my story and that of Allan Scott Family Winemakers in search of a blueprint for, or roadmap to, success, nor view the book as some sort of vanity project. Those who know me well are aware that I am my least favourite subject of discussion. Yet with each passing year that my wife, Cathy, and I have handed more of the family business's daily operations on to our children — Victoria, Josh and Sara — I have filled the emptier hours reflecting on my forty-plus years in the vineyards and winery. It seemed only natural to  document them. Whether I am the lead character, a supporting character, or just a character — in the most insulting meaning of the word — in the history of Marlborough is up to others to determine. All I can say for certain is that the full story of our family and our winery, as well as that of our region, has yet to be written.

The best is yet to come, I believe, and as you read this book between now and then, it is my expectation that you will gain a new type of enjoyment, understanding and appreciation of Marlborough wine and our place in it. Which is to say that, right at the physical heart of the Wairau Plain, is an honest Kiwi family who have always looked out for each other, tried our hardest for each other, and loved nothing more than emptying a few bottles and sharing laughs together. If that has resulted in a lasting business or a significant contribution to grape-growing and winemaking, all the better — but, for me, it's not what is most important.

CHAPTER 1

THE OLD HOMESTEAD

'IF THIS IS THE RIGHT THING TO BE DOING,' CATHY
said to me, 'shouldn't we be celebrating with a bottle of Champagne?'

It was the winter of 1993, nearing midnight. Cathy and I were seated at our long farmhouse-style kitchen table, which was piled high with dog-eared documents. Each was loaded with more incomprehensible legal jargon than the next. She and I gave each other that look every married couple knows: that most uncomfortable gaze that simultaneously says everything and absolutely nothing at all.

The cold weather didn't help our mood, even though most days during the Marlborough winter the skies are crisp and blue with bright sunshine. The vineyards below them are always a vast, depressing shade of brown at this time of year. The vines are dormant, taking a rest after having completed their months-long job of growing and ripening grapes. Even though workers pass through the rows and slowly transform the vines, one at a time, from tangled webs of shoots and branches into clean, pruned and perfectly positioned plants ready to return to life come spring, there is no sense of

27

relief until they actually do. Marlborough is eerily quiet, and with snow covering the imposing peaks of the Richmond Range to the north, you feel as though it will be a miracle if green, vibrant life ever returns to the valley. Of course, you know it always will — but at this particular time, Cathy and I felt as if we couldn't be so sure.

We were exhausted. All our lives we had worked non-stop, often holding multiple jobs between us, really with no plan — yet everything had eventually gone in our favour, despite the odd struggle or hiccup here or there. We had always muddled through and come out better the other side of any particular challenge. Victoria, our older daughter, was nineteen and soon to depart for London on her OE — that rite of passage for many young New Zealanders, the Overseas Experience. Our two youngest, Josh and Sara, were full of energy and excitement, and would be off to boarding school in Christchurch in a couple of years' time. And here we were, sitting in our house in the middle of our vineyard; our cellar door had opened for business across the street only a couple of years earlier. Everywhere you drove in Marlborough, vast new Sauvignon Blanc vineyards were entering production, many planted with vine cuttings that our company had grown, grafted by hand and sold to other growers and wineries. Our kitchen table sat right at the beating heart of an industry in which we had built our family and found a measure of success, having bottled 10,000 cases in our third year in business.

No one tells you that raising a family — along with running a family business and keeping both moving forward — more often than not feels like you are carrying a millstone around your neck. In our case, this was complicated by one simple, universal fact of the wine business: each year, the cost of grapes goes up and the price people want to pay for a nice bottle of wine goes down. Somewhere in the middle, a small family winery like ours — never mind the family itself — struggles to survive. We had finally hit a point where we felt as if we needed to try something new to make it all work, in order to have a thriving, enduring enterprise to pass on to our children. We needed that plan or strategy we had avoided developing for so long.

28

That is why we found ourselves where we did on this night, surrounded by stacks of paper — none of them more life-changing than the one that displayed our drying signatures, scribbled at the bottom just moments before. The document was a Memorandum of Understanding that would combine Allan Scott Winery into a public company along with Cellier Le Brun, Morton Estate and Regal Salmon Limited. The new venture would be a $16 million company — $25 million in today's dollars, accounting for inflation — called Appellation.

For some reason, though, popping a bottle of Earth's finest bubbly was the farthest thought from our minds. A small part of this had to do with exhaustion, but mostly it was Cathy's instincts — which were to be proved dead-on. Something simply didn't feel right about handing over control of everything we had worked so hard to build. Sure enough, a mere two days later we would learn that we had tied ourselves to a tanking company. The complex legal and financial entanglement designed to enrich and empower all of the partners, it turned out, would threaten to sink every business in the mix. We stood to lose absolutely everything — our brand, our vineyards, our home.

To anyone outside the industry, the wine business seems so simple: grow some grapes, crush them, let the juice ferment, bottle the wine, have a few laughs. While that's oversimplifying it a bit, in truth, it is only as complicated as you make it — and we had taken a swan dive into a labyrinth. Untangling ourselves from it would require six months of expensive legal and accounting work. Ultimately, we were successful in extricating ourselves from Appellation, and we regained control of our own family business. But by then the coffers were essentially empty, which meant we had to start all over.

Unfortunately, the series of steps we would take over the next few years, all focused on resurgence, would set us back yet again — and this time even threaten to put us out of business for good. But I often think back to that one night, and that particular moment in which Cathy voiced her concern that we might be taking a misstep since we didn't feel like celebrating. I know that no matter how difficult or expensive it was to undo the share float and get back to our own basics, the experience truly made us a stronger business and a stronger family. From that point forward, we learned to make better, smarter decisions in our personal and professional lives — and it's perhaps the most important of many reasons why our wine brand still exists.

The other reason I think back to that night so often is because it reminds me that everything Cathy and I have built, we have done so as partners — but she brings that extra, special element that's hard to quantify. Cathy has always had a sixth sense about things that I perhaps lack. Or maybe she is a more natural, better judge of character. Whatever it is, she has an intuition that is rare — and rarely wrong. To this day, I know that if ever there is a bottle of bubbles open on the kitchen counter when I arrive home from work, there's absolutely nothing to worry about.

Even now, I am somewhat amazed that I found myself in — and suddenly out of — a share float, considering where and when I had started: on a small farm near Waikari, in the foothills of the Southern Alps, about 16 kilometres from a town called Hawarden and about 100 kilometres north of Christchurch. It's really best described as the middle of nowhere, but in a good way.

I was born there in December 1947, as Allan Arroll Scott.

According to some, that is. It's hard to say for sure, because Waikari and Hawarden, each with only 300 residents at the time, weren't exactly renowned for their record-keeping. You registered births, deaths and marriages at the post office in Waikari, and you did your business and banking at the post office in Hawarden. When I went to get my first passport years later, as an adult, I first had to obtain my birth certificate from the

Me as a toddler on the family farm at Lancevale

postmaster in Waikari, who had written out the original document by hand. When I retrieved it, the postmaster informed me that my middle name only had one 'l', as in Arrol — not Arroll, as I had always thought. 'I have other bad news for you,' he said with a chuckle. 'You're illegitimate, since your father never signed and printed his name at the bottom!' So, at least as far as the state is concerned, the precise details of the very start of my humble upbringing are a bit murky.

And my upbringing *was* humble, no question about it. We lived in a small farmhouse on a property managed by my father, Ben. His father, Eli, had lost their nearby family farm around 1936, towards the tail end of the Great Depression. (The only justice here is poetic: the land our family owned is now planted with grapevines.) I think it was always a sore point for my dad, not having a home farm of his own. He was reminded of this daily, because the hills on which he worked and raised his family sat between farms owned by two mover-and-shaker farming families of the era, the Rutherfords and the Littles. The Little family is known to this day for having pioneered the Corriedale breed of sheep, which is a cross between a Lincoln and a Merino. Corriedales could be raised for both meat and wool, and thus became the most important breed in many countries around the world.

My father couldn't lay claim to anything like that, but I don't think he ever let it bother him that we were living in the proverbial shadows of the two prestigious South Island families situated either side of us. He just went about his business. (The bigger cross he had to bear was not having been able to serve in World War II, because he was a farmer and had sustained 'work injuries', which was the technical term for varicose veins, even though this didn't slow him down one bit. He never mentioned it specifically, but I always had the feeling that it weighed on him that he didn't make the sacrifices and contributions that others his age had made.)

Born in 1910, my father had worked his entire adult life as a shepherd and general farmhand. Shortly before I was born, he and my mother, Isa, landed at Lancevale — a separate holding, but once part of MacDonald Downs, a large sheep station in Hawarden. The aforementioned Rutherfords had previously owned MacDonald Downs, which in its heyday was sort of a South Island version of *Downton Abbey*. It was a huge, old homestead, with cooks in uniforms, maids who wore little hats, and even a kennel with hounds for the hunt. The Rutherfords were forced to sell the property in 1952, and it was subsequently split up. The farm I grew up on was a high, rolling 121-hectare section of the original 11,330 hectares, about 16 to 20 kilometres from where my dad first arrived in the region to work. He and my mother were able to raise me and my siblings there because my dad went into a partnership with the original owner of MacDonald Downs, who had sold the estate and then downsized to a rolling lowland property in Waikari, which he named Jedburgh (after the town in Scotland where the Rutherfords had come from). Together, he and my dad farmed both pieces of land — by putting us on one property and farming both in collaboration, the owner was essentially able to finance his investment in both farms.

32

Ours was situated right on the edge of Masons Flat, just north of Hawarden. The area is named for George Mason, one of the original settlers of the region in the 1800s. The farm and the house are still there — it is a beautiful, remote, peaceful area. As I get older and the more I think back to the time and place, the more I realise we had a pretty good life, even though it was extremely frugal; everything was recycled and reused because my parents had lived through the war, and the Depression prior to that. My mother even made hand towels out of sugar-bags. There were no real luxuries, but we never went without, either. My mother was a fantastic cook, so she always fed us up, and there were always cakes in the tin and monstrous meals — pretty much all protein and vegetables farmed by my parents. We cooked on a wood-fired stove that also heated the house, which was a pretty basic, square, standard structure for the time, sort of like a Railways house. It had two original bedrooms and a third one that we added later; there was a sitting room, and the main family room featured a coal range and a big farmhouse table around which we all sat. It was just us — our nearest neighbour was a kilometre or two away.

Like my elder brothers, Ken and John, and sister, Rosemary, before me, I helped out with all the chores and tasks on the farm, as we all were expected to do from not long after we could walk. The one thing my family didn't do, however, was drink. Part of the reason for this was that we were staunch Presbyterians, but back then drinking was also a form of élitism, really, since there wasn't much else to do if you had money and time on your hands, and other people to do your work for you. Dad would have a beer or a whisky around Christmas, or maybe a drink after completing a harvest, but that's about it. For those who did drink, the tipple of choice was gin; wine was almost unheard of.

However, one of my earliest memories was going into a glasshouse on the Jedburgh estate — and it had a grapevine in it. It was the most alien-looking thing, this gnarly plant with grapes hanging off it. I'm sure the vine was Albany Surprise, or some other hybrid variety, because the grapes were inedible,

Looking uncomfortable in my new uniform as I prepare for my first day at school

never mind useless for winemaking. They had that foxy flavour that burns the shit out of the back of your throat. They are sweet to taste at first, but then you swallow them and you practically choke. But the reason the vine was planted in the glasshouse is that, then, every farmer believed the region was too cold for growing grapes — which is funny considering how many millions of vines blanket that same area today.

As strange as it might have been for there to be a grapevine in that place and time, I have to admit that our neighbours probably thought our family was a bit out of place, too. I am not sure whether it was out of defiance, or a genuine interest, but my father decided to milk cows despite the property's 365-metre elevation and the fact that every farm in every direction for many kilometres raised sheep exclusively. Yet we milked cows. Every bloody day. It wasn't a big herd by today's standards, but it did feel a bit weird having them alongside the sheep.

One thing about my dad, though, was that when he set his mind to something, he excelled at it; and he was, in fact, a very good breeder of Friesians, sometimes called Holsteins. The award-winning cream was sold to a factory in Christchurch, and the neighbours would come each day and pay for a fresh bottle or jar of the milk. (My mother's father had been a cheesemaker, and later managed larger dairy and cheese factories, so between her and Dad there was nothing about cows they didn't know.) We had pigs and beef cattle as well, but Dad loved those Friesians like children, and he became quite well regarded as a good breeder of stock. That might be why, to this day, I hate bloody cows — other than to eat them.

Then again, raising cows just might have been my dad's way of thumbing his nose at the upper class that surrounded us; his way of doing his own thing, and doing it better. I should point out, here, that in the early 1950s, which isn't even that long ago, you knew your place and you didn't step outside it. My parents were definitely cautious, even subservient, but only with their words. Their actions, however, said everything about them — and you could see it with but one glance at the farm, which did all the talking. Certainly as a farmer, Dad was smarter and better than anyone around.

Even the untrained eye could clearly see how superior our land was in every respect — green and healthy, an absolutely thriving ecosystem. I wouldn't call it an organic farm, since the idea had yet to be fully understood or embraced in New Zealand, but that's basically what it was. (For me, as a kid at the time, it was a bit embarrassing that everyone else had a new motorbike or tractor, while Dad had a horse and a jogger. But he was so, so far ahead of his time, in that today's serious organic farms do things just as he did.) My dad never used chemicals of any kind, and ours was the only pasture in the area that could withstand a drought spell. The land was carved with deep gullies, most with willow trees growing out of them, making it fantastic cattle-grazing country. Those gullies retained moisture, and always had grass growing in them naturally.

In other words, when Dad was asked to work the property he probably only needed to take one look at the place to know instantly that it was perfect land for cows — he didn't care that I was embarrassed or that the neighbours laughed at him for his favouring cows over sheep. What's more, our stock never once contracted foot rot. It was like gonorrhoea rolling through the area some years, and yet our sheep and cattle were always the healthiest-looking — never small, malnourished or diseased. They always had a green, grassy pasture to graze, billowing with lucerne and alfalfa. There was even chicory, which many farmers regarded as a weed, but Dad knew that it had very high nutritional value for cattle, with its deep roots able to reach moisture far below the surface of the soil.

Grandfather Eli Scott's eightieth birthday, with, left to right, my cousin Brian Fraser, my siblings John, Rosemary and Ken, and me in my school uniform

Those gullies were also my greatest source of fun, growing up. There were other kids in the area, and after all of us had completed our chores we would spend hour after adventurous hour entertaining ourselves on the land. We built forts and huts out of whatever we could find. The Waipara River ran through the bottom of the farm, so we were always swimming during the warm months. My friends and I especially loved climbing a sheer, 10-metre cliff by the river. We would fall two attempts out of three, and always had bits of skin coming off our elbows and knees. That's probably why my legs are giving out on me today, but it was all worth it.

Seemingly every moment was worry- and carefree, for which I can thank my parents. There is a decade between me and my next-oldest sibling, my sister, Rosemary. I was a complete afterthought, and basically an only child, two-thirds of a generation behind my oldest brother, and so I was usually left to my own devices … and mischief. Unlike my parents' generation, which was class-driven, my friends and I didn't worry about being defined as anything less or more than anyone else. We could see and feel the change: that our world was to be what each of us made of it, individually, with nothing predetermined by where, when or to whom we were born.

I suppose that could have got someone like me in quite a bit of trouble. It did, somewhat, but my parents trusted me to learn discipline and responsibility on my own. This didn't make me a terribly attentive student in school, mind you. I dreaded every bus ride to Hawarden in the morning, especially in the cold months. The rickety bus had windows that were held up by a leather strap with a hole in it, which you would attach to the frame. It wasn't long before the leather would wear through, and the window would then always be open during the slow, cold ride. The school itself was just like the pioneer schools you see in old films, with students ranging in age from five right through to high-school age, all in the same building.

At a Hawarden Secondary formal dance, c. 1960: left to right, Tony Moore, Chris Williamson, Rick Warwick, me and John Williamson

Hawarden Secondary School, c. 1963. Back row: Stewart Jamieson, me, Chris Williamson; front row: Rick Warwick and Doug Eavies. Doug had just been appointed a school prefect.

Right away, my teachers could see that school was not the right place for me. I was comfortable there, but I was also easily led, so I could be inattentive, lazy and disruptive. Part of the reason I could never stay focused was because the lessons didn't challenge or invigorate me; again, something for which I can thank my parents, my mother in particular, who was a voracious reader. She kept everything, especially the newspapers, so I read what she read. Both she and I were hungry for knowledge, but I also expanded upon everything I read. For example, while other kids in school were just beginning to learn basic arithmetic, I could go through the papers and work out problems I had made up for myself — the percentages of boys versus girls in the birth announcements, the types of trucks for sale and the percentage discounts on them. I know, it's a bit odd, but it's what put me ahead of the class in some respects. I knew what was going on in the news, too. My teachers tended to get annoyed with me, because I already knew the answers to their questions, which meant I couldn't be bothered with the lessons most of the time.

My friends picked up on this very quickly. Granted, I wasn't the best at choosing my mates, most of them being poor students, good athletes, or a combination of the two. They were hopeless with schoolwork regardless, and would ask me about what was being taught. It inflated my ego, of course, and made me even less attentive.

I have always told myself that I was simply drawn more to the idea of working and making a living than to studying in school. But, looking back, I think it is more likely that Mum and Dad inadvertently inspired me with their hands-off parenting. I am still a bit of a bookworm to this day, always eager to learn something new; I also picked up my father's work ethic. Every day I was in a hurry to rush home from school to make a buck somehow. Whether it was shooting rabbits for a 2-shilling bounty per rabbit, or plucking the wool from and burying a dead sheep for Dad (which was the worst job in the world, by the way, but he paid me well for it), I would do it. I never was at the stage where I wanted to leave school, though, and

39

On my bike, at my parents' farm, setting off to play club rugby

in truth part of me wishes that I'd had more interested parents who would have pushed me harder academically. Then again, there are some choices we make consciously and deliberately, and others where we simply have to do what feels right in the moment. And my decision to leave school at the age of sixteen was more or less made for me.

While it is true that I felt as if there wasn't much else to learn at the Hawarden school (and there probably wasn't), my parents were ready to retire and travel. My mother had always had wanderlust, and having worked all their lives my parents decided they would spend their remaining active years on the move, financing their travels by spending short stints looking after farms for families who had gone away on holiday. I was self-sufficient – and left behind.

A few months later, my older brother John came back to the farm to take my father's place. He had been working for several years as an engineer for a transport company, and was ready to settle down with his wife and raise children. They built a new house on the property and picked up where Dad

The Waipara River skirted our property. Enjoying a dip there are my niece Anne Reveley, me, my sister-in-law Vera Scott with daughter Alison, my sister Rosemary with daughter Jeni, and Rosemary's husband, Graham Reveley.

had left off, except for the part with the cows — my brother gave them away. But he spent the next several years becoming one of the region's foremost organic farmers.

I, however, had to make my own way, armed only with my mother's thirst for knowledge and my father's work ethic. I didn't go particularly far, at first — only to be a farm labourer on a property nearby that needed someone to take care of the land and live in its two-bedroom house. The job paid a paltry £5 10s per week (of which the 10s went on board), but I enjoyed the structure and sense of satisfaction I found in a day's work. I stayed there for the next three years, playing rugby after work, and spending each day climbing the 1,000-metre hills, working with the stock, repairing fences, shearing sheep, and — I hate to say it — milking the damn house cow.

I DIGRESS ...

It seems to happen in every family business: the founder, after several years at the helm, becomes less the guy who makes big decisions and more the one who wanders around telling stories and sharing experiences about the good ol' days. It is fair to say that I still contribute, and often I am able to identify and scrutinise details or elements of the business that others cannot. But at the same time I enjoy being able to regale the winery and vineyard staff with tales of my rather fortunate — although often strange and silly — life.

One story I tell fairly often has to do with choosing your mates wisely, because you never know when and under what circumstances they will arrive on your doorstep. My best friend growing up was a fellow from a nearby farm. We were born only four days apart. His family was very similar to ours, too — they were skilled farmers, but also very obviously more intelligent and aware than almost everyone around them. Each and every member of the family was successful at whatever they chose to do later on.

My friend and I, however, always managed to get into some measure of trouble, especially as we got older and got around on our own. After we had left school, we not only worked together, but we would drive into Christchurch on the weekends to hit the bars and parties. We only diverged when it came to drugs, and around the time that The Beatles began to transition to psychedelic rock with the release of *Rubber Soul*, my friend discovered a passion for just about any hallucinogenic substance. I never took drugs, so I often wound up being his minder. It didn't bother me; I was always happy to do it, and we always had a good time on the town.

What I didn't expect, however, is that he would disappear to India. To say he had gone troppo was putting it mildly, I thought, as I didn't hear from him for more than thirteen years. Apparently, he had settled in near the Tibetan border and become a Hindu. I never expected to see him again.

Then, in the late 1970s, when our daughter Victoria was only three or four years old, she came running inside to tell us that a strange man was walking up our driveway, carrying a pumpkin. I went outside to find that it was my childhood friend ... carrying not a pumpkin, but a sitar, as well as a massive crayfish in his knapsack.

My friend had returned home to the farm where he had grown up, near my childhood home, and had walked the entire way from there to Blenheim — all 260 kilometres of it. I guess he thought it unwise to show up empty-handed, so somewhere near Kaikoura he had bought the crayfish. Not that I didn't appreciate the thought, but it was the middle of summer, so needless to say both he and the crayfish were a bit whiffy.

After a badly needed shower, my mate filled me in on everything he had seen and done in the past decade. He entertained us for the rest of the day with lucid — if somewhat strange — tales of everything he had experienced (often under the influence). What amazed me most was that, beneath the layers of the strange clothes, the strange stories and still stranger smells, he was still the same intelligent, thoughtful fellow — just a bit more of a hippie.

I lost touch with him again soon after that, but I later learned that he returned to his family farm and got on with his life there. I love his story, not just because I grew up with this fellow, but because it's quintessentially Kiwi: grow up, find yourself abroad no matter how long it takes, return home a better person.

Although I suppose the other moral of the story is to be sure that your mates get home safely after a night on the town. At the very least, a decade or more down the line, there might be a smelly, sunbaked crayfish in it for you.

CHAPTER 2

THERE SHE WAS – AND AWAY I WENT

I RECKON IT'S SOMEWHAT NATURAL TO ADMIRE OR be envious of old married couples who can recount an engaging, romantic tale of when and how they met. For all the things Cathy and I do have, this most certainly isn't one of them.

For a start, she and I were both seeing other people when we were set up on a blind date at a mutual friend's birthday party in Christchurch in 1967. What's more, we both pretty much had our bags packed. Cathy, who had been flatting with her sisters and working in an office in town, was scheduled to move back home to Blenheim in a couple of weeks' time to start a new career in nursing. And, after a few years on the farm, I was bound for Australia with my rugby mates, Doug and Dougal, for an OE. Neither Cathy nor I was exactly on the prowl, and to make things especially awkward I had to explain to her why I was limping around like an idiot, my knee thoroughly wrapped in bandages.

It was February, the time of year when everyone on the South Island is outside, enjoying the warm weather. A few nights before the party

Me around 1963

in Christchurch, I had gone to the Hawarden Ewe Fair — about as exciting as it got in rural Canterbury in those days. A friend of mine was throwing a party at his house afterwards. We were swimming in the pool when my friend's sister took exception to something I said or did, and she chased me out of the pool, onto the deck. I slipped and caught my knee on the edge of the concrete path, spoiling what would otherwise have been a good time. It hurt like hell, and I winced with every step I took for the next couple of weeks. Even now, I'm certain that at first sight of me Cathy believed her friends had set her up with an utterly incapable goof. All I could do to convince her otherwise was simply to own up — and admit that I had sustained the injury while being chased by a naked girl.

Mind you, this wasn't exactly a regular occurrence. Neither Cathy nor I spent our prime years trying to capture the attention of the opposite sex. She and I function so well together, in fact, because we both value our independence. Growing up I had one friend who shagged everything that moved, as well as another who took his options (and probably did shag around more than I knew of), but I never went to sleep worrying that I hadn't got a root that night.

I suppose that this was a bit unusual in the freewheeling, laid-back spirit of Christchurch at that time. When my friends and I would drive into the city on a Friday night, it seemed that almost everyone was looking for the three Fs. It was the height of Beatlemania, everybody was in an imitation Beach Boys surfer band, and the Monkees hit 'I'm a Believer' was playing on constant loop at pubs and parties thrown by the nurses or the agricultural students at the university. Worry-free as life was, however, everyone still hadn't quite come out of their shells, and people tended to retreat to groups of their own kind in pubs or drinking holes. My friends and I were sort of the oddballs, since we were rugby-playing country boys who dressed and talked a little differently to everyone else in the room.

I was perhaps the most country of all my friends, in fact. My boss was quite an accomplished farmer named Jack Denham, an intensely dedicated man who had developed my work ethic even more than my parents had to that point. He and I spent day after day working in remote areas, building or repairing fencing — he was absolutely pedantic about doing it right, making the fence straight and solid. Until I began working for Jack, I had believed that I had a clear and comprehensive understanding of what it meant to do a day's work, but I quickly learned that, by comparison to Jack, I was a bit 'rip, shit and bust'. Jack showed me the importance of the finishing touches. If you are fencing up and down hills, as we seemed to be doing to infinity, you have to put the appropriate fixtures in place in the humps as well as the hollows, otherwise the wire will snap and fly down the length of the fence. That only has to happen to you a couple times, leaving you to work your way back to the beginning to start all over again, before you realise the importance of resisting the temptation to take shortcuts. You do things once and do them properly, lest you waste your time.

That was the sort of thing that occupied most of my thoughts at this time in my life (along with rugby, of course). So I can't say with any clarity or confidence what I might have said to Cathy, at that party where we were introduced, that would have interested her, or vice versa. Of course, I do get a smile when I think of trying to dance with her to 'I'm a Believer' with my leg in bandages. I guess that Cathy and I saw in each other that aforementioned sense of independence, as well as a drive and ambition that was a bit rare among people our age. She was going to Blenheim, where she had grown up, to do her own thing; I was headed to Australia to do mine.

49

Cathy (right) with her older sister
Frances, Christchurch, 1965

A couple of weeks or so later, Cathy and her flatmates came to Lyttelton to see off me, Dougal and a couple of other mates who would be setting sail for Australia. Again, I can't lay claim to some sort of romantic send-off, even though Cathy and I both admit that there was an unspoken connection of sorts between us. The thing that stands out most, actually, is the memory of Jill, Dougal's girlfriend and a flatmate of Cathy's at the time, just sobbing uncontrollably as we boarded the interisland ferry for Wellington. She cried and cried for him as if he was going off to war. Cathy and I, on the other hand, merely agreed to stay in touch as best we could via letter, and left it at that.

It's easy enough to remember that there were no text messages, emails or Skype in those days. But it is worth mentioning that communication was truly a challenge, so my expectations regarding staying in touch with Cathy weren't terribly high. The idea of going to Australia felt like visiting another planet; no one I grew up with or knew had ever even been to Auckland. Right up until the 1970s (some would even argue the 1980s), visiting the North Island was like going overseas. So just taking the overnight ferry from Lyttelton to Wellington was a big deal for us.

We couldn't possibly have felt further from home than shortly after we boarded the vessel that would take us on the three-day voyage from Wellington to Sydney. We went straight to that ship from the ferry, and once we were in open seas the bar was open twenty-four hours. It was only mid-morning when we set off, but, as any Kiwi knows, nothing good can come of a 24/7 bar and young, rugby-playing guys away from home for the first time. The bar served Carlsberg, which was completely alien to us, but we loved it — up to that point, we had only drunk Ward's Best Bitter or Canterbury Draught. (We would never have thought of transgressing by supping North Island brews such as Waikato Draught or Wainuiomata Bitter.) That day, we had a pretty good session, one Carlsberg after another. Although we knew our limits back home, on land, none of us knew what higher-alcohol beer would do to us at sea — and the Carlsberg was very strong in comparison to what we were used to. Since I'm a bigger-framed fellow, the alcohol didn't hit me quite as hard, so I stayed in the bar and kept at it as other people slowly disappeared and evening approached. This would prove to exacerbate what would become a truly awful situation once the North Island had rolled off the back of the horizon.

The swells were *massive*. It would have been bad enough if our bellies weren't already full of Carlsberg, but the boat started rising up, up, up … and DOWN. Over and over and over again. It was a force of Nature unlike any our bodies had ever felt. All of our years of smashing into each other on the rugby pitch didn't compare in the slightest, and everyone became sick almost instantly. There were four of us to a cabin, and when I returned there from the bar I found all three bunkmates in agony. Dougal was curled up on his bunk, his face as green as the trees. I just burst out laughing — the sight of him in such a state nearly killed me. I felt sorry for him, but the Carlsberg wouldn't let me express it, and all he could do was mutter 'Fuck off' between heaves into a bedside bucket. I remember thinking that, even though the room smelled absolutely putrid, I could handle it … until my stomach suddenly rumbled as if it were the Tasman Sea itself.

I ran to the loo, and commenced what would be a three-day marathon of me shitting and my three mates vomiting. Non-stop. As soon as one person ran into the loo, another would be waiting. Sometimes there would even be a queue. It didn't stop until we reached the harbour in bright, sunny Sydney. We couldn't get onto terra firma fast enough, all of us sore to the point that we felt as though we had been doing sit-ups the entire duration of the journey. The relief we felt upon stepping on shore is one I sometimes recall fondly, although I won't ever shake the instinct to laugh whenever I see a Carlsberg. It's a shame, because I rather enjoy drinking it, but the brand is forever associated in my mind with the sense of agony and suffering it contributed to those horror-filled three days.

We were able to hit the ground running in Sydney, though, quickly shaking off the traumatic sea voyage as only the young and wide-eyed can do. It was our first experience in a big city — and it was massive. None of us having been even to Auckland, Sydney was truly impressive. For a couple of days we took in the sights, sleeping in a pub by night, but we couldn't dally. OE for us was nothing like what it is for young Kiwis exploring the world today. For us, there was no travel for the sake of travel, or developing a sense of cultural enrichment. We had to work or go back home — actually, it was work or starve, and we also needed to save money for a return ticket. Our OE was on a shoestring, so the four of us who had traversed the Tasman Sea quickly went our separate ways.

Dougal and I hitchhiked our way to Moree, a small town on the way to being as far north as you can get in New South Wales before you reach Queensland. At first we rode on the back of a truck, which dropped us near Newcastle. Next, we were picked up by a caravan-driving older couple who seemed to stop at every pub along the way. As we weren't the legal drinking age of twenty-one, we would wait in the van, roasting in the open-sky Australian heat while they drank comfortably indoors — although occasionally they would bring beers out to us. When the couple dropped us off in a town of about ten people, most of the way to Moree, they asked for our parents' addresses so that they could write to them to let them know we were alright. Imagine my mother's surprise, receiving a letter from these strange people, and wondering what the hell was going on.

After standing on the side of the road for what felt like ages, we eventually got ourselves a ride to Moree. Dougal had arranged work for himself in advance, and went to meet his contacts. I went to the local stock station to see if they could find me a job. Right away they put me onto Gurley Station, a nearby wheat farm (today it is planted with cotton). The manager, it turned out, was on his way into town anyway, so he picked me up in Moree and took me out there — to the middle of absolutely nowhere.

This was desolation on a scale I couldn't have possibly imagined, with dirt roads pointing to different parts of the horizon — and still less than nothing beyond there. The town of Gurley, if you can even call it a town, was about 15 to 25 kilometres from the station. I don't remember seeing a house or any other sign of civilisation in Gurley, no matter how simple. Although, this being Australia, of course there was a pub. (For some strange reason, there was a guy who always sat at the corner of the bar with a sack that held a huge snake that he'd take out and show to anyone who asked, then place it carefully back into the sack.) But that was it.

Now, few can claim to have ever heard me whinge about working. But toiling on a massive wheat station on the hot, exposed plains of New South Wales for tiny wages was truly awful. I wouldn't wish it on anyone. The fields reached as far as the eye could see. There were all sorts there — jackaroos, truckers, tractor drivers, you name it — and we all lived together in a basic, uncomfortable boarding house with communal showers. We slept in what looked like prison cells. The building comprised but a small part of a big compound, which also had a cookhouse and sheds for about twenty tractors, bulldozers and combines. Each day you got up and had breakfast, then walked across to the yard. The foreman would assign jobs, and off you went until your shift was done for the day.

My first week was miserable. I was put on the stick-picking crew, which was mostly made up of local Aboriginals. This gang was given the unenviable task of following the grubbers after they had ripped up the bush. We would walk in long lines behind the grubbers, picking up all of the timber that could potentially get caught in the next wave of machinery to roll through. We would then put all of the debris in piles and set them ablaze, sending black columns of smoke twisting into the sky. Thankfully, because I had done farm work for most of my life, I was assigned to drive a tractor after a short time.

Still, the work was as tedious as it was monotonous. To be sure, vineyard work often is as well, but at least it results in a quality end product! This was just seemingly indiscriminate scarifying, and getting the paddocks ready for wheat while curious emus, kangaroos and foxes looked on. Each day seemed hotter and dustier than the one before, probably because the pay wasn't particularly good (although it was slightly better on the night shift, which I often worked). And the job was antisocial. Today, I am not exactly renowned for my skills with glad-handing and small talk at marketing events or tastings, but I still require at least some contact with like-minded, rational humans. Here, there were none to be found, and because I didn't have a car I was at the mercy of others to do something as simple as visit the pub in town. There were a couple of Kiwi guys working on the station whom I could relate to at least a little bit, but the highest form of entertainment was an old fellow with a pet galah that would roll over, play dead, walk up a tree — pretty much anything it was commanded to do. Beyond that, we were starved for basic interaction or entertainment.

About the only fond memory I have of the place was trying to help one of my workmates dispose of a burnt mattress. He had fallen asleep while smoking a cigarette and had singed a hole in the mattress, which in this place felt like it was equivalent to a jailable offence, as our pay was docked for the most minor of infractions. To help our workmate avoid a penalty, we figured the best course of action was to dispose of the evidence — but we weren't terribly capable conspirators. We were frustrated to the point of giggling as we tried to stuff and squeeze this rigid, uncompromising mattress into a car; had there been a witness, they would have testified that we looked ridiculous and incompetent, or perhaps plain drunk. At some point we managed to get out of the compound with the mattress, but it just so happens that it is much more difficult than you'd think to dispose of a mattress discreetly in the middle of the night in remote New South Wales. In the end we dumped it on the side of the road and decided to plead ignorance as to its whereabouts, although we would never learn whether that was the best option. Before the bosses could get in a snit over the missing mattress, a scrap broke out between the Aussie and Kiwi workers over God knows what. Some punches were thrown and the foreman got rid of the lot of us.

He was doing me a favour, of course, even if I didn't realise it at the time. Unfortunately, only worse opportunities lay around each corner for the next several months. I took to pumping petrol at a service station that was also a garage that sold used cars. This seemed a good fit at first, since the owner quickly realised that I could count. He was terrible at keeping his books, so he moved me to the office. I wasn't much better at bookkeeping than he was, but I could manage the accounts well enough that the business ran smoothly and I could nick as many cigarettes as I liked. Anyone could see, however, that this wasn't a good place to settle down by any means. The garage owner's lack of basic mathematical skill was in fact his most endearing quality. He was a cruel, brutal, mean, miserable bastard who sold dodgy cars to anyone down on their luck, particularly Aboriginals. Then he would repossess the cars when the people couldn't meet his outrageous payment terms. The biggest, nastiest guys would come looking for him, and one time he gave me a baseball bat and told me to hide behind a door, to wait in case things got out of hand. Thankfully, I was never needed to perform any such services, but I felt it best to move on.

I quit the job and moved to a flat in Moree, where I had a stint working in the spare parts department of a tractor dealership. I found the work to be duller than I could have imagined, but nonetheless I rather enjoyed my few months in Moree. My flatmates and I lived in a big, communal house of sorts, the best part being our next-door neighbours. They were world travellers who would tell us story after captivating story about places that none of us could even have located on a map. (The place they loved above all others was Afghanistan.) I was only in the house for a few months, but I can certainly say that I grew up quite a bit in that time.

At Sydney airport on my way back to New Zealand
after nine months away, 1967

It turned out that one of our flatmates was gay, which was something I had heard of, but never actually believed existed. When one of the other flatmates told me about it, I remember thinking to myself, 'People do that? It's a real thing?' Funnily enough, it didn't bother me in the slightest. My first instinct was that maybe I could help him. After all, what better way to cure someone of sexual confusion than to take him to a rugby game? So that's exactly what I did, and I can't for the life of me imagine what he must have been thinking at the time. I lost touch with him after I left Moree, but I hope that, wherever he is, he is still raising belly laughs and tears among his friends and family when he tells and retells the story of the young, naïve Kiwi farmer boy who thought that establishing sexual preference was a simple matter of seeing a rugby match!

One good thing about a return to civilisation was that Cathy and I could begin corresponding. While I am sure a letter could get to Gurley nowadays, back then it was impossible — maybe you could deliver it via a bank branch, but the closest bank I could use was in Sydney. But Cathy and I could now share our thoughts and experiences, and we began exchanging letters every few weeks. Communication became even easier after I moved to Sydney to stay with my cousin, whose husband, Pete, had offered me a job.

Now, if I thought I had seen mankind at its worst at the Gurley wheat station, I can't say that I saw us at our best when I started working with Pete, who was a wildlife officer for what was then called the New South Wales Fauna and Flora Protection Panel. Most of the work involved covering a wide expanse of territory, writing out permits for kangaroo hunters. That part of the job was fine: just driving around in beautiful, remote areas, sometimes sleeping in the back of a station wagon under the stars. But one time he handed me off to spend a week working with a professional hunter. The guy had a sliding window and, on the door on the passenger's side of his truck, he had affixed a padded rack mounted with a .243 rifle equipped with an infrared scope. He drove, and I was the trigger man. It was absolute slaughter. I would just put the red light on the head of the kangaroo and pull the trigger. All night long this went on, him driving and me shooting, then the two of us would gut and hang the kangaroos on the hooks of the Land Rover. We would get back at 2 am, covered in blood and guts. The night crew would process the carcasses, and by the time we returned in the morning our work clothes and the car would be spotless. As gruesome a job as it was, at least every part of the animal was used. But if anyone wonders why I don't complain much about my work nowadays, this experience pretty much sums it up.

Nevertheless, I'd had about enough of Australia after nine months. As luck would have it, I received a letter sent by a shearer from near where I grew up: he wanted to quit and was offering me a share in his shearing partnership. I had saved enough money for a return ticket on a 707, my first-ever commercial jet flight, and booked myself a trip home.

Cathy in the late 1960s

I arrived back in Canterbury to find that relatively little had changed — except that I knew Cathy would be a part of my life from then on, one way or another. It wasn't terribly easy at first, as I dedicated every waking minute to my new job, and she was busy with her new career, nursing in Blenheim. Yet I was able to move into my parents' old house, since they were still travelling the countryside, and I could start on my life again. It would take a while yet before Cathy and I would settle down, however, as our shared ambitious and independent natures were just starting to show.

I DIGRESS ...

If there's one type of animal I seem to be at odds with more than any other, it's the house cat. I don't know what it is, but cats never seem to be able to survive in my presence. Let this be a warning to all cats: I have nothing against you, but your odds are most definitely not in your favour when I happen to be in the vicinity.

The first time I became aware of this was about six months after Cathy and I had married. We were living in the house on the farm near Hawarden, and Cathy got a couple of kittens right after we moved in. They absolutely loved Cathy, and would snuggle up to her for attention, but they always steered clear of me, acting somewhat suspicious. I just dismissed it as the usual sort of feline moodiness or unwarranted cynicism.

One night my friend Rod, from up the road, had driven by to pick me up for rugby practice. It was that time of year when the sun sets right about the end of the workday, so, even though it was still early evening, the sky was already black.

'Come quick, get your gun — there's a possum outside,' Rod said as soon as I opened the door to greet him.

In case you don't know, the common brushtail possum is perhaps the biggest ecological disaster ever to hit New Zealand. The species was introduced from Australia in the 1850s for food and the fur trade, but our country proved the perfect habitat for the animal's explosive reproductive rate and insatiable appetite for native plants of just about every type, as well as for ground-dwelling birds and their eggs — including the precious, endangered kiwi.

At night anywhere rural in New Zealand, which is pretty much everywhere, you can see possums up in the trees. Their large eyes, having evolved for nocturnal foraging, immediately glow like beacons if you shine a spotlight up into a tree, but you will also see these fox-like creatures along the side of the road, foraging for grubs and plant matter. A general rule of thumb is that, if a possum happens to be on the road, its saucer-like eyes glowing in your headlights ... take aim and hit the accelerator. You're doing the country a favour.

As if all that weren't bad enough, possums carry and spread bovine tuberculosis, which is one of the worst nightmares for any farmer raising beef or dairy stock, as I was at this time. So it was with haste that I turned and ran inside to grab my shotgun, and instructed Cathy to close the door behind me. She was happy to do so, as she had already come to expect the worst behaviour from me and Rod after we had shot a possum or two. One time, Rod picked up the warm corpse by the tail and twirled the animal around a couple of times before letting go — accidentally sending it into flight. The possum hit me square in the chest, leaving a large splotch of bright crimson on my light-blue shirt. It looked as though I was the one who had been shot — and Rod's eyes just lit up. 'Quick, lean up on me. Put your arm over my shoulder,' Rod said, grinning. 'Cathy, come quick!' he yelled. 'There's been an accident!'

'NOT FUNNY!' she screamed at us after she realised we were cracking up.

Now, if you don't have a spotlight handy, the next best way to hunt a possum is simply to listen. The animals have big, talon-like claws that allow them to dig deep into bark and scurry up thick tree trunks. Before ascending a tree, a lot of the time a possum will dig its claws into the base of the trunk, making an unmistakable, spine-tingling, scratching, crunching noise. But Rod and I had a torch, so we began shining its beam around the base of all the nearby trees, looking for that haunting glow of eyes and the sound of claws scraping and digging into tree bark.

Eventually I heard some rustling in a hedge near the base of a tree, and shone the light at it. There was the silhouette of a possum, its front legs outstretched and reaching up, ready to make a quick ascent. I took aim and …

BOOM!

Now it has to be said, I'm not a particularly good shot, mainly because I despise hunting, whether for sport or for food. While I understand the appeal, outside of the paddock or shed, killing animals of any type, for any reason, is something I would prefer someone else do. Granted, we were on a farm, where possums are a most unwelcome sight, which for some reason, this one time, made me an expert sniper. I blew that little bastard possum to smithereens. One shot, job well done.

We walked up to the hedge and Rod aimed the torch's beam at what was left of the possum … only to see that it was one of Cathy's cats. Rather than trying to climb the tree, it had simply been using the trunk as a scratching-post, and had paid the ultimate price for its accidental and unintentional mimicry of our nation's most destructive critter.

Now, most people say that the first year of marriage is the hardest. This is true, but just try throwing into the middle of that twelve-month period the accidental slaughter of your new spouse's beloved pet. Poor Cathy was devastated, to say the least, and I am amazed that she elected to stick around and resisted the temptation to give the remaining cat to someone far away from me. Rather fortunately, though, it went on to live a long, healthy life, in large part because Cathy did her best to keep it inside. However, perhaps following Cathy's lead, I got the sense that the cat was always giving me the evil eye, and its instinct would be proven to be spot-on over the next several years. I wish it weren't so, but, when it comes to cats, I'm pretty much the worst thing to happen to their species since rabies.

CHAPTER 3

ALL WORK, NO PLAY

SO₂ 11/2/16

MERCUREY
FRANCE

ALLAN SCOTT
FAMILY WINEMAKERS

15P32

GC

THERE HAS ALWAYS BEEN THE WAY OTHER PEOPLE
do things, then the way Cathy and I choose to do them. Early on for her, it
was starting a career at a young age in New Zealand in lieu of opting to do
an OE, as all her friends and her five sisters had. For me, it was always trying
to be a little bit better at my job.

Through 1968, along with some forestry work, breaking in some rough
areas with a bulldozer and some basic tractor driving, I was shearing sheep
whenever an extra set of hands was needed. It is hard, unforgiving work. To
shear the standard 200 Corriedales per day, you would start on the dot at 7.30
am. You would shear non-stop for an hour, have a five-minute smoke, then
get back into it again until around 9.30, when the farmer's wife would bring
around fresh scones, biscuits, cakes and tea. The work was hard on your back,
so you'd just sit on a bale of wool and have your cup of tea for half an hour,
not wanting to move an inch. Then on the dot of 10 you would get into it
again for an hour, have a quick break for a smoke, shear some more, then at
noon you would take an hour for lunch at the farmer's house, which was a

ABOVE LEFT: Demonstrating shearing in 1993 — the last time I did this
ABOVE RIGHT: A sketch I made of myself when I was shearing in Australia

nice, solid meal — usually a cold roast and spuds. You would work for another hour, starting at 1 pm, go have a smoke at 2, and at 3 pm take half an hour for a cup of tea and scones, then work from 3.30 through to 5.30.

At that point, most people would pack up and go home to do the tally, since you were paid by the sheep, but I often took on extra tasks. One of the older, wiser shearers taught me an early lesson: that if I could find a way to move things along faster or more efficiently, I should do it, even though shearing time is manic at most farms. The weather is uncomfortably unpredictable, hot and dusty one moment, cold and rainy the next; the dogs are barking; and everyone is struggling to keep up. Unless we were under pressure and falling behind (shearers' language gets even more offensive than usual under such conditions), I would take five minutes away from the clippers to stand at the gate and help draft — that is, sort the sheep and direct them towards the different shearers — which saves an enormous amount of time down the line. While this would make me down two sheep on the tally, it would ease the pressure on

Cathy in Sydney, 1969

everyone else. Or I would wait back at the end of the day to help the farmer fill the shed or take the other small steps that would make the following day easier for the entire operation. (Sometimes the sheep I would lose on my tally I would get added back on for doing the extra work, or sometimes the farmer would send me home with mutton.) Even at mealtimes I would wait in line, and not push in and join anywhere as almost everyone seemed to; I would even put scraps in a pile and stack dishes rather than just leave them. Some probably thought I was old-fashioned, but I was just acting on the lessons instilled in me by my parents and by Jack, my first boss.

On Friday afternoon, the work week didn't end for me. I was spending my weekends in Blenheim, and, although the main reason to drive up from Canterbury each Friday night was to see Cathy, her dad, Arthur Morrison, always seemed more excited than her by my arrival. He was a stock buyer, who would spend Monday to Friday buying stock and lamb and selling off the progeny and ewes; and each weekend he had about a month's worth of work stacked up for me, everything from shearing sheep to killing muttons to drenching cattle. Since all of his children were girls, I more or less became the skilled, unpaid farmhand he had always wanted to have around. I would drive back down to Canterbury on Sunday night, then go straight back to work Monday morning. It was gruelling, but I rather enjoyed working with Arthur. I would do the donkey work, certainly, but I learned quite a lot from him. More importantly, I knew I had a mentor who had my well-being in mind.

It wasn't long before Cathy decided to move down to Christchurch to be closer to me and gain more nursing experience in a bigger hospital. While that didn't surprise anyone, what did is that she and I decided to go to Australia together not long thereafter. I wasn't in a hurry to return there by any means, and our parents were a bit taken aback by the decision since we weren't married (although we were engaged). But Cathy's sister was doing her OE in the Northern Territory, and Cathy wanted to visit her.

We weren't gone for very long — maybe six months in total — and we didn't see each other as often as we would have liked, much less cohabit. From the time we started in Sydney, to and through our time in Adelaide a couple of months later, I did every imaginable job — builder's labourer, bricklayer and car washer, to name a few. We eventually went up to Alice Springs, although I spent much of that period in bed, having been hit with the Hong Kong flu. The pandemic killed about 1 million people towards the end of the 1960s, and it took me weeks to shake it. During much of that time Cathy and her sister were preparing and cleaning houses at Pine Gap, an Australian–American spy base in the desert outside Alice Springs. As I recovered I began looking after a caravan sales yard next door; a job that essentially required me to do nothing but regain my strength, since anyone remotely considering buying a caravan would just hear a line of bullshit from me, and then go away. Eventually we returned to Sydney and did the last thing I wanted to do: take the boat back across to Wellington. Fortunately, on this voyage the seas were calmer, I avoided the Carlsberg, and Cathy, her sister and I returned to life as it had been before our departure.

On honeymoon at, appropriately, Honeymoon Bay, Golden Bay, Nelson

It was late 1969 when we arrived back in New Zealand, and Cathy and I married in a ceremony at her parents' home in January 1970. In order to get started on our lives, we had to begin building up a nest egg, so we went back down to North Canterbury, where I could shear sheep. The timing was actually somewhat fortuitous, as the owner of the shed where I had worked in the past had sacked the Maori gang that had come down from the North Island to work. I teamed up with my mate Bruce, with whom I had sheared for some time beforehand, and we put together our own gang of shearers at MacDonald Downs. The pay was better and I started to gain management experience. More importantly, I learned relatively quickly that I was much better at organising shearers and shed hands than actually shearing. We kept

Helping Arthur (wearing the hat) and his farmhands with the cattle

the operation running for about two years, which allowed Cathy and me to have a fairly comfortable, happy life at home in a rural farmhouse.

It was a somewhat lonely existence for Cathy, however. She had put her nursing career on hold for those couple of years, and spent most of her time keeping up our house, the vegetable garden and our chickens. She enjoyed being at home, but she hated the solitude. Our nearest friends were a few kilometres away, so we didn't see them very often. Also, I would be knackered when I got home from work, and what little spare time I had was dedicated to playing rugby. Generally, we were starved of excitement. Everything changed, however, when we got the news that Arthur, Cathy's dad, had suffered a mild heart attack. He was getting to the age where he probably realised he couldn't do everything on his own, yet he wouldn't admit it to himself until he had that health scare. So Cathy and I decided that I would set aside the clippers for good, and we would leave Canterbury so that I could help Arthur in Blenheim. Oddly enough, even after those couple of years of loneliness in Canterbury, Cathy bawled her eyes out when we finally packed the car at the beginning of 1972 and watched the farmhouse disappear from view out the back window of our car.

To be perfectly honest, though, Cathy's solitude and Arthur's ticker weren't the only reasons I needed to switch things up: shearers don't exactly occupy the highest rung on the social ladder. There is not any particularly good reason for this, mind you, since it is an honest, hard day's work. But nobody throwing a dinner party thinks to invite the bloody shearer. I don't get particularly bothered by that sort of thing usually, but it was clear that I had become *persona non grata* purely because of my profession. Cathy's mother was quite prim and proper, and I imagine that a shearer didn't quite fit her ideal family model either.

We were quite lucky in that we weren't just any young couple arriving in Blenheim for the first time, looking for work and a place to live. Arthur was quite successful in his work, so he had been able to buy several properties over time. He allocated a 10-acre (4-hectare) block to each of his daughters, on which they could build houses for themselves and their families. (While this might seem extremely generous, and it was, it's worth remembering that at this time a single acre (0.4 hectares) of land cost a few hundred dollars.)

Our property was off Old Renwick Road, a pretty spot with a view of the Wither Hills. As soon as we possibly could, we built a house — and to finance it, we got to work. Cathy started nursing at night, and I begrudgingly dug out the clippers to shear for anyone who needed it. In those days, lots of people had a few sheep on their property, but no idea how to shear them, so they would call me. There was also a big factory up the road that manufactured pellets for chicken and stock feed — known among the locals as the Lucerne Meal Factory — where I did every job from cutting and drying lucerne

71

Drenching cattle on the back of a truck

to driving trucks (the latter was my primary responsibility). I would help Cathy's dad during the day, do some shearing after that, then head to the factory to start at 4 pm, finish at midnight, then go home and get some sleep.

It was around this time that I discovered I had a green thumb. To make extra money, we ripped out the lucerne growing in the paddock next to our house and started contract-growing vegetables for seed, as well as pine trees for forestry plantings. If you drive by the race course on Old Renwick Road today and look across the street, you will see massive pine trees reaching into the sky — I planted them all around our house (which is still there), and to this day I feel a bit of pride when I pass them on my way into town. Pines were in demand, particularly by people planting forestry blocks in the Marlborough Sounds, but we also developed quite a following for our garlic and our seeds. Although, I must say, the process of seeding tomatoes is messy, sloppy and time-consuming — maddening, even. We were under contract to deliver 10 kilograms of seeds per year, which doesn't sound like a whole lot until you consider that you need about 300 seeds just for 1 gram of weight. Growing, separating, drying and preserving 10 kilograms of seeds is a *lot* of tedious, mindless work. You only get a few minutes into it before you realise that you would rather spend your time doing pretty much anything else. However, over time it became clear that all of the work I was doing driving trucks or shearing sheep was supporting my true passion, which was growing plants. For the first time that I could remember, I had found something to do that wasn't just about paying the bills, but was work I actually enjoyed doing.

The transition wasn't easy or quick by any means. For many months to come, I would still be switching back and forth between jobs each day, about my only release being rugby. In addition to driving trucks at the lucerne factory, I was doing the winter maintenance work there: pulling apart, greasing and replacing pieces of the machinery with which the factory tried to extract protein from the plants. It was messy, miserable work that I hated with a passion, and each night when I got home there was more work to do on our small farm, particularly weeding between all the pine trees and vegetable plants. We worked so much that my first two years in Blenheim are essentially a blur.

However, there was something special happening in Marlborough in the winter of 1973, right under everyone's noses. For a short time, just as winter was setting in, Cathy's parents and one of her sisters decided to travel overseas for several weeks. I took over things for Arthur while they were gone, and, to be perfectly frank, the most exciting thing to me during that time was that the Marlborough Rugby Club was having an extraordinary season. The team was about to head to Christchurch to play Canterbury for the Ranfurly Shield, which happened to coincide with the return of Cathy's parents and sister. Just before we were to drive to Christchurch to pick them up (where I would try to convince Arthur to go and see the match), the news broke that hundreds of hectares of land in the Brancott Valley had been sold to a mystery buyer, for the wide planting of some mysterious crop. Soon, Arthur and I were watching many of my friends from the Marlborough team hoist the shield in triumph. Even though the excitement of that game was of a kind I won't soon forget, my memory of it is somewhat overshadowed by the discussion Arthur and I had over what could be happening back home. By the time we had returned to Blenheim, the rumour was out that Montana Wines had purchased nearly 1,200 hectares of land in the span of about a week and a half, about 400 hectares of which would be planted immediately with grapevines.

I knew absolutely nothing about wine, but the notion of growing fruit to produce a different product entirely was absolutely intriguing, given all the time I had spent to that point tending to my own small farm, growing every vegetable we could think of to make an extra dollar. Wine played absolutely no role in our lives — I'm not even sure if I had tasted wine to that point, much less knew where to buy a bottle.

'You know,' Arthur said to me, 'there just might be more of a future in it than driving a truck and shearing sheep, especially over winter.' I admitted he had a point. And then he sealed it: 'And you're not enjoying what you're doing.'

So I agreed that I should look into a job. I didn't know where to begin, but, as it turned out, Arthur took care of that before I could.

Several years before, Arthur had worked as a stock auctioneer for Pyne Gould Guinness (today better known as PGG Wrightson, the agricultural-supplies behemoth). One of the employees he had hired was John Marris, a local then renowned for his youthful ambition. While most know John for the Wither Hills winery, founded by his son Brent in 1992 and later merged with John's land holdings, John came to the wine industry through Montana's purchase of vineyard land in the Brancott. Along with his stock-agency work, John gained real-estate qualifications shortly before Montana came calling. It was John who helped Montana acquire the land it needed to establish its wine empire — and it was John whom Arthur rang about finding me a job on the vineyard.

'Sure,' John said to Arthur. 'Send him round on Monday morning. Have him drive up to the big barn and ask for the manager on-site, Jim Hamilton.'

It was early August, and word had it that workers were already pulling down the fences on the newly acquired lands. I drove out there very tentatively, and it seemed there were a million other people there, all of whom had been promised or already allocated jobs. I realised that it wouldn't have mattered if Colin Meads had placed the call in lieu of Arthur: anyone and everyone was as needed as they were welcome.

I stepped out of my car, and began wandering towards the barn, in search of Jim. I only expected to do a day's work and earn a day's pay. I had no idea that showing up then and there, on that cold, blustery day, was the decision that would change everything for me and for my family, much less cement my place in a global industry.

I DIGRESS ...

Everybody has their flaws, and I am rather embarrassed about the one of mine that is most well-known to my family, friends and business partners around the world. Although it is something I can't help, it is a source of amusement for others, and usually, when enough time has passed after each incident, I am able to laugh as well. As funny as you might find this and the other related situations I will describe later on, please do know that this is rather difficult for me to write about. But here goes ...

Sometimes, I simply cannot stay awake.

There could be cannon warfare in the next room, and yet I will still manage to nod off in some of the most entertaining or important social or business-related situations. It's not slow, either; it's sudden. One minute a sentence will be rolling off my tongue, and the next minute — gone. Even during the time I was working with my writing partner on this book you are reading, I would doze off occasionally. It wasn't as if we were discussing an uninteresting or boring part of my life, either. I would be recalling a particular story or detail about my youth, my time working in Marlborough's first large-scale vineyard or even my children, and ...

Zzzzzzz …

I usually snap out of it after half a minute or so, but sometimes the spell will last longer. What usually happens, if it is a social situation, is that I will fall asleep mid-sentence when I am talking about one particular thing, then, when I wake up a moment later, finish the sentence — although I will be talking about something else entirely, as if someone has hit pause on me, then fast-forward, then play. (One time, for example, I was talking about lawyers, nodded off, and then awoke talking about Martians.) My close friends and family know this about me, and are able to laugh it off or snap their fingers or cough; I then snap back to, apologise, and life goes on. However, it is a bit startling and even worrying when I doze off in the presence of strangers. They usually don't know what to think or how to react, as happened, for example, with a Canadian distributor I was travelling and working with, who feared I had died — I came to with him checking for my pulse.

My problem is usually exacerbated when I make a brief visit to another country for a distribution meeting or a wine dinner. Let's just say it leads to some awkward moments around the dinner table when the guest of honour, who has flown for eighteen or twenty-four hours just for this one event, is talking about the Marlborough terroir one moment and then, the next, has his head back, his eyes closed, his jaw slack, and lets out a wall-shaking snore.

Nowadays, I usually go out of my way to schedule meetings at times of the day and in places where I am least likely to nod off — especially if I am travelling abroad. This is because one of the first times I experienced a bout of narcolepsy — if that's indeed the nature of my problem, although no doctor has ever said so — was also one of the silliest.

Cathy and I had travelled to London for a series of meetings with our UK distributors. They were a small family company, like us, and we got friendly with them over the first couple of years in business together. On this particular trip, they invited me and Cathy to have dinner at their home, along with about half a dozen other guests — all nice, pleasant people, and supposedly important in the wine industry.

We had just arrived in town, however, and, between the combination of jet lag and general exhaustion, I was struggling to keep up with the banter around the dinner table — and eventually, I started struggling to stay conscious. With each morsel of food or sip of wine I raised to my mouth, I felt exponentially more bloody awful.

I was trying my hardest to fight the all-system shutdown procedure my body had set in motion, when one of the other dinner guests invited me into a side conversation about something that, I'm sure, was quite a sensible, normal topic of dinner discussion. Then I was asked a question by another of the guests, somebody's wife, and midway through answering her …

Zzzzzzz …

When I came to a few seconds later — which probably felt like hours to this prim, proper English lady — I started talking about poisoned rabbits.

Yes, poisoned rabbits.

I have no idea what we were talking about before I slipped into unconsciousness, and I have even less of a clue how that had anything to do with little furry animals having ingested harmful chemicals.

Everyone stopped what they were doing and looked at me. Forks were suspended mid-air, heads were tilted slightly askew, and faces were wearing expressions of complete bewilderment as if, collectively, the room was asking me, 'What in the hell just happened?'

Cathy, of course, was beet-red. She didn't know whether to ignore it, explain what had just happened, burst out laughing, or change the subject. She often does try that last approach, but on this particular occasion I didn't leave her a single opening. What was she supposed to do? Interject with, 'That is absolutely true about those little buggers, bloody poisoned rabbits. I have had about enough of them, I tell you!'?

I suppose the lucky thing is that people are always polite with me about it. They never say, 'What the fuck are you going on about?' They just look and smile at me. I usually realise right away what has happened, and instantly I get this unmistakable feeling of 'Shit, I did it again.' And typically at these kinds of gatherings, people eventually drink enough that, later, they only recall having had a fun and delightful evening. So this time, like most others, I managed to hold it together through the rest of the meal, and just get on with it as if nothing had happened.

Zzzzzzz …

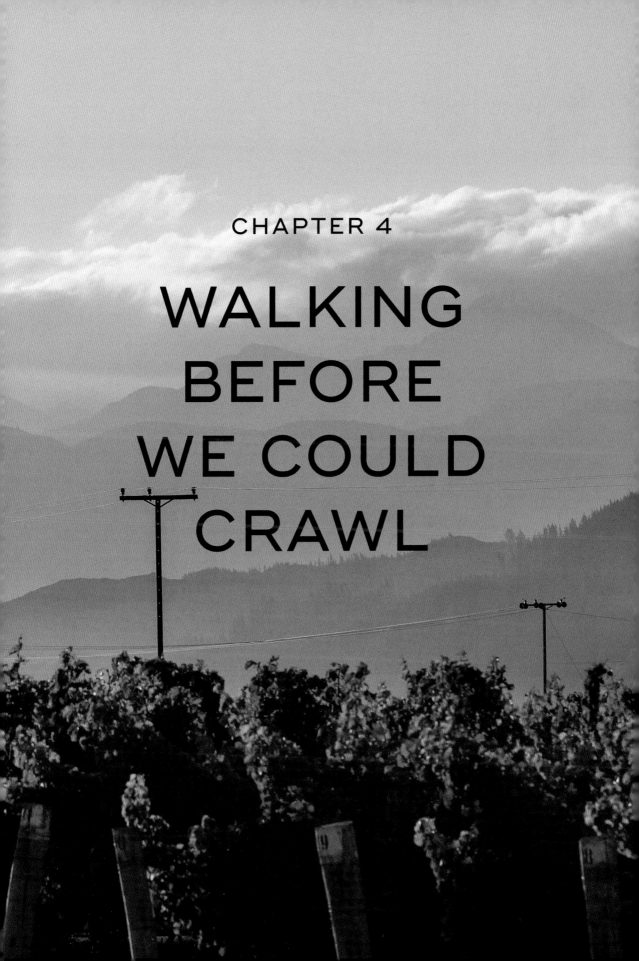

CHAPTER 4

WALKING BEFORE WE COULD CRAWL

'SECRET'S OUT,' I MUMBLED, STATING THE OBVIOUS
as I drove my car up to the Waldron family's property for the first time in August 1973 — a place soon to become known as Brancott vineyard, even though the Waldrons were still living in the house and the property had yet to be paid for fully by its new owners. There were about eighty or ninety locals milling about, many of them already having been assigned tasks for the day or the week, and others still waiting. I was late for work, as I often am even today. (I tend to get distracted with tasks around the house from the time I wake up at 5 am, and, before I know it, the workday has already started for everyone else.)

This might be why, after I met Jim Hamilton at the reporting station, he sent me to find someone on the property named Graham, who would tell me where to go and what to do. I walked up to the fellow I assumed was Graham, and he said, 'No, no, I'm not Graham. See that guy down the other end?', as he pointed towards a tiny figure in the distance who was leading another small group of workers. 'That's Graham down there.' So I plodded

Making an early start in the Brancott vineyard, c. 1974: left to right,
Jim Hamilton, me, Andy Solly, Roger Banks and Philip Sutherland

all the way across the rocky, weedy terrain that had been trodden only by hooves for decades. I approached the managerial-looking man who had been indicated about five minutes prior.

'Hello, Graham?' I asked, breathing hard from the long walk. 'Allan Scott. I was told to report to you.'

'Me? No, I'm not Graham.'

'Shit, really?' I asked, feeling somewhat small. 'So who are you?'

'I'm Clive,' he said. 'Graham is the guy you were talking to down the other end.'

I slumped my shoulders and turned to walk back towards Graham, who seemed to be sporting a bigger and bigger grin the closer I got to him. Only a few days old, and the Marlborough wine industry had already embraced the tradition of taking the piss out of the new guy.

When I reached Graham the second time, he assigned me to the planting line. I was to spend the next few weeks pushing vine cuttings into the hard ground, wondering what on earth I had done, giving up my shearing clippers.

It was freezing cold, the wind was whipping across the plains and, perhaps worst of all, nobody appeared to know what they were doing. Everything seemed to be decided on a whim, with no plan other than to rip down the fences and just get these little sticks planted into the ground as quickly as possible — splinters that looked as if they would never grow to become anything, much less grapevines. Over the next several years, I would learn from many of my co-workers in those early days that the general sense of disarray and confusion about all aspects of this place wasn't just an inkling, it was real. There never was much of a plan at all, not a soul had a clue what they were doing or why — so it's a miracle that the Marlborough wine industry ever got going to begin with.

That Clive fellow I had been sent to speak with, Clive Drummond, is one of a few gents I consider to be among the true founding fathers of the Marlborough wine industry, along with Dick Simpson, Wayne Thomas and Jim Hamilton. None of these guys have their names emblazoned on grandiose wineries or millions of bottles every year. The four of them are never mentioned in *Cuisine* magazine spreads or in textbooks or on wine tours. Only a tiny percentage of people who drink New Zealand wine here at home or the world over have even the slightest clue that they exist, much less have heard their names mentioned by others. Yet the legacy of what we know as Marlborough more or less starts with these guys. Sure, they all worked for bigger players: namely Frank and Mate Yukich of Montana, and their ambitious real-estate agent — and eventual administration manager — John Marris. But for all the combined money and influence the Yukich brothers wielded, nothing could have got even partway started if not for the contributions of Clive, Dick, Wayne and Jim. (It's also worth noting that John Marris's office assistant, Sue Smith, kept everything meticulously organised to such a degree that everyone would have been hopelessly lost without her.) In particular, I view Jim Hamilton as the most important contributor — and also as my mentor with all things viticultural.

Now, Montana Wines is New Zealand's largest wine company, but it had humble origins, like many of New Zealand's established wineries. In 1934, Croatian immigrant Ivan Yukich had planted grapevines in West Auckland's Waitakere Ranges, and ten years later he began selling his own wine. In 1961, his sons, Mate and Frank, established Montana Wines, which later became a public company and now operates as part of French wine and spirits giant Pernod Ricard.

Jim Hamilton began working for Montana in 1967, when his family sold its farm in Mangatangi, near the Firth of Thames, just southeast of Auckland. Jim was sixteen years old at the time, his father had recently died, and the family felt it best to sell their land to an expanding Montana. Suddenly in need of work, Jim asked for and received a job on one of Montana's largest vineyards — a 49-hectare block that produced a large percentage of the company's total grape output. Jim, as inquisitive and smart as he is practical, was made a leading hand within a few weeks, and a foreman after a year. He became a manager after four years, and was promoted to national vineyard manager early in 1973.

Not long after harvest that year, Jim was taking a badly needed holiday in the Bay of Islands. He had left his cheque book at home, however, which he discovered at the end of his stay when he realised that he couldn't pay for his motel. So he rang the Montana office, asking if he could charge his stay to the company and reimburse the expense upon his return. Montana couldn't have cared less.

'Oh, we were wondering where you were,' said the office assistant at the other end of the line. 'You'd better come home — you have to go to Blenheim on Monday.'

After Jim had raced back to Mangatangi, south of Auckland (about a five-hour drive), his first order of business was to look at a map to find out just where the hell this Blenheim place was. After that, he packed a bag and caught a flight south, where he met up with Frank and Mate Yukich. With the brothers were John Marris and Wayne Thomas, who arguably deserve as much credit for Marlborough's wine industry as almost anyone.

Wayne, a consultant who had studied agriculture at Lincoln University, was the first to suggest to Montana that it consider Marlborough for its expansion. He had examined several options in Gisborne and Hawke's Bay, but every property he found was either too small or too expensive (or both). Then Wayne found several decades' worth of weather data from Woodbourne, where Blenheim's airport sits today, and concluded that Marlborough, while dry and susceptible to the occasional spring frost, was sunny and had the free-draining soils that might suit grapevines nicely.

John Marris showed Frank, Mate, Wayne and Jim thousands of hectares' worth of properties in just a few days, and by week's end he had secured 1,173 hectares, in three locations, on all of which Frank had paid deposits out of his own pocket. The group returned to Auckland but, shortly after their arrival, Frank was turned down by Montana's board when he asked the company his father had founded to pay for the rest of the land.

Of all the people I have ever met, Frank Yukich is the most determined, the most motivated, the most hardheaded. When he sets his mind on something, he never quits until he gets what he wants. Usually his heart-on-sleeve ambition inspires others, but many suspect nowadays that Frank had never imagined that the board would derail his Marlborough expansion plan — the typical charm offensive would be enough. It was only after he supplied a technical report written by Wayne that the board approved the purchase.

Frank was also incredibly hardworking. Jim and others who worked with Frank closely would recount his typical work schedule with a sense of awe: arrive at his vineyard near Auckland by 7 am, work twelve hours, then go to his office to do paperwork for another six hours, go home and sleep a couple more, then get up to do the same thing the next day. So it is no surprise to me that he fired from the hip on Marlborough. I say this because, even armed with Wayne Thomas's weather research, the decision to plant grapes on the spots of land he acquired was based on the absolute bare minimum of knowledge and information. Maybe even less. But Frank was the sort of guy who viewed challenges as obstacles you just attack over and over again until you are met with submission, all other opinions and information be damned.

You realise this all the more when you consider how Dick Simpson found himself in the Montana fold. At the start of winter in 1973, he was just a guy with a big tractor. He was a self-employed agricultural contractor, aged thirty-seven, who owned a Ford County, then one of the biggest and most powerful tractors on the market — and, according to Dick, at the time he owned one of only three in the entire country. In the middle of June that year, the local Ford dealer rang Dick and asked him to drive his equipment to the Waldron property to provide a demonstration. Dick had no idea what this was all about, or who the people were who wanted to see him in action. At this point, it was still a secret who had purchased all that land.

Dick arrived at the appointed time and place, and began ripping at a small corner of the Waldrons' farm, moving the dry, rocky earth with relative ease. He was the first to report that morning, and he would be followed by two other teams demonstrating their International and John Deere equipment, respectively. The onlookers, whoever they were, seemed most pleased by his performance. Dick showed that he and his tractor could cultivate the land in any manner the new owners desired, readying the dirt for planting with just about any crop. Dick believed he would get a call at any moment to begin work, but his phone never rang.

Dick Simpson clearing trees with his Ford County, 1973

Fortunately, he knew John Marris, having purchased supplies through John's employer, Pyne Gould Guinness. Dick went to see John to ask why he hadn't been hired. Clearly, his Ford County had proved superior, had it not?

'No tractor is being hired,' John told Dick. 'They want to do it all with their own machinery.'

Dick, as it turned out, had auditioned his equipment, not himself. He didn't know that he had demonstrated his tractor's prowess for representatives of Montana Wines, who, following the performance, sauntered into the Blenheim Ford dealership seeking to buy a dozen County tractors of their own. Two weeks later, the dealer still hadn't procured all of the desired equipment (it wasn't sitting there in a showroom, as we expect nowadays), and, once John explained that his client was waiting for the desired tractors, Dick offered his business and his tractor for sale.

'Deal,' John said, without hesitation.

Then and there, Montana Wines owned Dick Simpson's tractor and all its compatible tools. For $1.75 per hour, Dick was to begin clearing Montana's new properties.

While most people think of Brancott as the origin of the modern New Zealand wine industry, it was just the largest of the three farms Montana had acquired in Marlborough. In addition to the Waldron property that would become Brancott, there was also the Renwick Estate, previously known as the Gill property, and the Fairhall Estate, previously owned by the Walsh family. Dick would break the ground at all three.

There are two things worth noting at this point in the history of New Zealand wine. First, clearing this land was a nightmare of a task for Dick, since not only was it a dry year, with less than 25 centimetres of rainfall, but Montana's new properties had never been considered as suitable for anything other than grazing. This meant that they were rocky, uneven and practically billowing with lucerne, an incredibly resilient plant that has evolved to survive drought. Its roots can reach 15 metres below the soil, so just scratching it off the surface rarely kills it, which is why it is ideal for pasture land. (And this was long before the days of species-specific agrochemicals and weedkillers.) All of this is just to give an idea of how unsuitable this land was for planting grapes — and yet Frank Yukich wanted every inch of Marlborough he could possibly purchase. Second, and perhaps more important to our industry's story, is the speed with which Dick was bought out and put to work, because it speaks volumes about why Montana's arrival in Marlborough was executed in such a clandestine manner — and a hasty one at that.

Today, if you own a large sheep paddock next to a vineyard at the heart of a world-renowned winemaking region, anyone who wants to buy your land likely wants to grow grapes, not sheep. So you can charge a premium for the property. But in the early 1970s, before grapes were a proven crop, inflated prices weren't quite the same barrier to entry for Montana that they would be for a buyer in the here and now. Certainly, if landowners had known that Montana was looking for property, they might have raised

Purpose-built vine sprayers made at the vineyard

their prices, but they didn't, and land was so abundant and undervalued that much of it could be had for $50 per acre ($20 per hectare). The average price in the region was about $300 per acre ($120 per hectare), and, even though Montana wound up paying well above market rates, the company could have afforded to pay plenty more. Montana's problem wasn't financial, it was cultural.

Almost everyone in the area had stock as their livelihood, and farmers believed that any new crop coming to the region would alter the existing usage rules and regulations for fertilisers, hormones or general land management. If your family has been working a piece of land, raising stock on it successfully for generations, the last thing you want is some guy moving in next door, altering the productive balance of the region — let alone the new guy telling you what you can and cannot do with *your* business because of what he wants to do with his, even though you have been there forever. Also, Marlborough was, and still is, a small, intimate place in which almost everyone knows each other — so if you are Montana and John Marris, you know that the farmers will tell all of the contractors, such as Dick Simpson, not to work with you. Not only will you have a hard time finding land to buy but, once you own it, you will have hundreds of hectares and no one willing or able to help you farm it, so you will be losing money all the while unless you have equipment of your own.

That explained the secrecy, but the haste — considering that Marris found all three properties for Montana in roughly a week and a half — and all the ensuing missteps on the land itself remain somewhat of a mystery to many, especially considering that Montana had Jim and Wayne on its core team. The truth is, Jim and Wayne, while smart and dedicated, were never given the necessary amount of time to establish for certain whether Marlborough in general was a good move, never mind the specific properties that Montana acquired. They had done no more than eyeball the land, and yet Frank and Mate had committed to spending $1.3 million on it with no clear knowledge of how to farm the properties successfully. Most accounts portray Frank and Mate as visionaries who foresaw a shift away from medium and sweet box wines to sophisticated, dry table wines and a booming global market for them. Bullshit. They were smart, but there's no question that they were taking a punt. Today, some people even suggest that Frank and Mate were taking a calculated risk of a kind most of us can't comprehend — that they were paying a small price to raise a large amount of capital through a share float. I like and admire Frank and Mate immensely, but they always were the smartest guys in the room. That is perhaps why some posit that the brothers knew that Montana could fail in Marlborough and yet protect themselves or even benefit financially, as if they were the viticultural equivalent of *The Producers*.

Look at it this way. You own a company, and you want to go public and raise investment capital on the open market. The way you do this is by demonstrating to investors how rapidly you are expanding to meet unprecedented demand for your product. But how? Well, how about by planting some massive vineyards as quickly as possible, and using them as a visual representation of how exciting an investment opportunity your company is? Seeing is believing, and no investor would think to ask the most basic, straightforward question: *This is high-quality land, and all those little sticks in the ground are going to grow up into big, productive grapevines, right?*

If you knew that the Yukich brothers were seeking a big investment at the time, and you knew how entrepreneurial and clever they were, then it made perfect sense that they would act quickly and quietly at first, spend a little over $1 million on land and not really fret whether grapes would actually manage to grow in Marlborough. And, sure enough, they had sold 40 per cent of their company to Seagram shortly before they arrived in Marlborough, and towards the end of 1973 they issued 2.4 million shares to the open market and raised $8 million — quite the handsome return on investment. That's all before a single grape had grown — and, arguably, one never needed to for Montana to make out very, very well.

Only Frank and Mate know for sure what their strategy truly was, and, even with the experienced advisers they had working for them, no one can deny that the Marlborough wine story is dumb luck. And it's also why those first days planting the land were laughably inept. In fact, you could argue that Montana's gamble on Marlborough paid off not because of the parcels of land they chose or the varieties of grapes they picked, but because, in choosing Marlborough, Frank and Mate just happened to choose a group of people who would make them successful.

Dick needed a solid month, working every day, to prepare the land before Jim Hamilton arrived at Brancott alongside John Marris. By now, Jim knew all too well where Blenheim was on the map, as he would make a permanent move and settle in as one of the key people in charge of putting the Yukich brothers' plan in motion. John introduced Dick and Jim, then let them get to work.

By the time I arrived a few weeks later, with about one-third of the Waldrons' fences already pulled down and a few hundred hectares cultivated, even my untrained eye could see how dry and inhospitable the dirt was. There was no denying that this was going to be a Herculean effort, and perhaps a futile one at that. Successfully planting this massive property might be one of the biggest Pyrrhic victories in the history of New Zealand agriculture, for all I or anyone else knew.

The mere notion of planting massive vineyards felt absurd, too, for the simple reason that most of us living and working in Marlborough at the time never drank wine. Some of us working on the soon-to-be vineyard had never tasted wine even once. There were only a few brands — Montana, Corbans, Selaks, Nobilo and Delegat's — and most of us wouldn't have been able to name them from memory. New Zealand had no wine culture whatsoever, really; wine was just this stuff that some people, mostly folks we didn't know, bought a box of now and again. It was relatively sweet, some of the boxes were labelled red, others labelled white. There were pretty horrific-tasting ports and sherries, too, but really nothing had the potential to taste good, since at the time there was no law requiring that wine be made of 100 per cent grapes.

Such ignorance and unfamiliarity is impossible to imagine today for anyone visiting, living in or working in Marlborough, possibly even for Kiwis in general. Today, even a person who is aware only that Sauvignon Blanc is white and Pinot Noir is red knows far more than we knew back then. Those were foreign-sounding names that few, if any, of us on the vineyard in 1973 had even heard before. And we sure as shit couldn't pronounce them. Even older, productive vineyards around Auckland and Gisborne were complete hodgepodges of different varieties — beyond Riesling, Sylvaner and Müller-Thurgau, all of the workers, up to the foremen and the managers, were in the dark as to what they were growing or why.

Not only were we all clueless, but nobody could agree on anything. Some thought that the land hadn't been cultivated deeply enough, others thought it was just fine. But really it was bone-dry, and no one was thinking about irrigation (least of all me). I was just a planter; I kept my head down, stayed

Graham Bulfin used a rifle sight to check the straightness of the planting line.
(Fairfax Media NZ/*Marlborough Express*)

quiet, did what I was told, and tried to learn a thing or two. Not that this environment was at all conducive to education at first, because everything was being made up as we went along.

Today, if a new vineyard is being planted, weeks of soil and weather analysis go into determining which varieties to plant. Lasers are used to mark out perfect, straight rows. The vines are either potted plants, already several months old, or cuttings grafted onto rootstock that is not only resistant to phylloxera, but is matched to the soil type.

At Brancott in 1973, however, there were stacks and stacks of crates containing cuttings, all piled at one end of the vineyard. All of the cuttings

Once the line was straight, a flag would go up to indicate that planting could begin. (Fairfax Media NZ/*Marlborough Express*)

had been soaked in insecticide, summer oil and god knows what else up in Gisborne, then packed into containers marked with strange words such as 'Müller-Thurgau', 'Cabernet Sauvignon' and 'Pinot Noir'. About eighty of us took part in the planting. We were each given a bucket full of cuttings, and told to stand in a long line. A cable, about 400 metres long and marked at 1.8-metre intervals, was stretched in front of us; one end of the cable was attached to a peg in the ground, the other to a tractor. A guy at one end, with a rifle and a scope, would look through and give hand signals to a few people in the line, who would move the cable in response to the signals until the cable appeared straight through the scope. A flag would go up from the signaller, and everyone standing in the line would kneel down, push a cutting into the hard ground next to their mark on the cable, then step forward 3 metres and wait for the cable to move again. We did this all day, every day, for weeks. As improvised and ridiculous as the system was, the rows were surprisingly straight. The problem, however, was that we were slow, never mind that we were planting sticks.

'This is crazy,' Jim would say to Frank Yukich multiple times during the planting. 'These things are never going to grow.' Frank would brush him off, telling him not to worry, and that Wayne would find a solution for any problems that arose.

Clive Drummond remembers an even bigger problem: communication.

Montana

PLANTING OF THE FIRST VINES

WAIRAU VALLEY ESTATES
MARLBOROUGH NEW ZEALAND

FRIDAY, 24 AUGUST, 1973

The programme for the official opening of Montana's first Marlborough vineyards, then known as Wairau Valley Estates

When so many people are trying to work together, relatively little gets done. It seems logical that the more people you throw at a task, the faster it will move towards completion. In the vineyard, however, it was the exact opposite.

'How many vines did you plant?' Clive recalls one worker asking another.

'Fifteen.'

'Really? Wow, I only did ten.'

Jim Hamilton at the ceremony (Fairfax Media NZ/*Marlborough Express*)

With each person planting only two vines per hour at most, it was going to take us years to finish. After the first few weeks, workers began disappearing due to the cold, unforgiving, howling winds that seemed to penetrate every layer of clothing. Then the school holidays arrived, and still more workers vanished. By the middle of September, we had gone from about ninety workers to a core group of about a dozen. But what surprised us all the most was that twelve of us could do better, faster work than ninety people.

Father John Sloan blessed the planting, watched by Montana executive Terry Dunleavy, a future CEO of the New Zealand Wine Institute, and a large crowd. (Fairfax Media NZ/*Marlborough Express*)

As the weather warmed and kinks in the processes were ironed out, we practically flew through row after row. We were suddenly planting hundreds of vines per hour, and by the time spring finally set in the dirty dozen of us had finished the planting at all three vineyards.

The next major issue to untangle was just how the hell we were going to get water to these thousands of new plants. The managers seemed to be putting a plan together over the next several weeks, with more equipment, trucks and large tanks arriving at each of the three properties. As this continued, Jim asked me to take a ride with him in his car, a Ford Falcon. We drove from Fairhall to Brancott, Jim taking those ten minutes or so to

Dignitaries at the ceremony included (left to right) Mate Yukich, Joe Babich (Babich Wines), Lyall McLauchlan (Marlborough District Councillor), Jim Hamilton (with head turned), Warwick Bruce (with beard), Alex Corban (Corbans) and Frank Yukich. (Fairfax Media NZ/*Marlborough Express*)

explain that Montana would be looking for more blocks of land. This meant he would be spending most of his time identifying and surveying properties, as well as organising people and equipment. Therefore, he would need someone to run a crew and, in particular, manage the watering of the new plantings while he was otherwise engaged. He needed someone to organise the disorganised — and he wanted me to be a leading hand.

Any pride I might have felt evaporated the instant he dropped me off at Brancott, where all of the workers were having a water fight in the warm, spring sun. One guy was wearing a wetsuit, splashing around the inside of a massive plastic water tank. There's nothing worse than being one of the gang, and then suddenly you're the boss.

The Brancott, Fairhall and Renwick properties were still nothing more than large plots of brown dirt with sticks protruding from the dry earth every metre or so. Although I had kept quiet up until now and had simply followed instructions, I figured it was time to start asking questions, and take the extra steps I had taken when I was a shearer to get things done better, faster and smarter. The only problem, of course, is that grapevines are far more temperamental, finicky and unpredictable than even the moodiest sheep — which is just one of many things that would conspire to slow progress over the next few years.

I DIGRESS ...

While I consider Jim Hamilton to have been my mentor in the vineyards, it was Frank and Mate Yukich of Montana who showed me (and countless others) what it truly means to be ambitious ... and also a little nuts. They were relentlessly competitive, too — and not just with other wine companies. If one brother knew that the other planned to start work at 7 am, he would arrive at 4 am. But what made the heirs to Montana special wasn't that they were the first to bring commercial grape-farming and winemaking to Marlborough; it was simply that they understood the power of their product in a way that few others could.

Probably their only equal in this respect was American vintner Robert Mondavi, who rose to prominence in Napa, starting around the same time. Much like Montana in New Zealand, Mondavi was always looking for a new angle to exploit with a sceptical public, long before anyone truly took Napa wine seriously. And quite like Montana in the early 1970s, Mondavi also made pretty mediocre if not terrible wine. What he lacked in winemaking knowledge, Mondavi made up for with his understanding of human curiosity, and of the price people are willing to pay to have it satisfied.

One of the tricks he employed to bring visitors to his cellar door was to drive up and down the two-lane road near his Napa winery at about 25 or 30 kilometres an hour, just to build up a parade of cars behind him, each new driver more annoyed than the next. When Mondavi reached his winery, he would slow down even more, signal, then turn in. Mondavi correctly assumed that anyone stuck in a queue of cars would ultimately make the assumption, 'If that strange guy has been driving so slowly along the road looking for this winery, there has to be something good about it, right?' Inevitably, several of the cars would follow him, come in for a tasting, and buy some wine. Others would follow suit, thinking something exciting was happening at that place, and they shouldn't miss it. Mondavi never quit dreaming of ways to lead lemmings directly to his doorstep.

Frank and Mate were just as driven, but Frank was the brainy, calculating one, while Mate was the more gruff, practical guy, who liked his forklifts, big trucks and bigger tractors. I am a fairly big fellow, but Mate was just massive; his hands were beastly. Calling him a man's man is putting it mildly. Despite the fact that he was rich beyond the dreams of most mortals, he just loved his truck and any piece of heavy machinery that he could attach to it. Together, Mate and Frank were truly the brawn and the brains, respectively, yet they shared a mutual passion for conquest and domination.

Not long after Montana had established a foothold in Marlborough, Frank asked John Marris and Jim Hamilton to hire a boat for him out of Picton. It was an odd request on an otherwise normal workday, but they did as they were told. Together, the three men drove from Blenheim to the wharf at Picton, where Frank instructed the owner of the boat to take him and his two deputies out a couple of kilometres.

'Stop right here,' Frank said, after they had been cruising into the Marlborough Sounds for a few minutes, Picton shrinking behind them.

If you have never been on a boat through the Sounds, you have no idea how majestic Nature can be. The water is a pristine, perfect blue, and the steep bush-clad cliffs either side are a deep, dark green. Even though the interisland ferry, cruise ships and cargo vessels pass through there several times a day, there remains a feeling of purity about the place. To many, it is one of the most beautiful, relatively unspoiled spots in all of New Zealand – which meant nothing to Frank.

'I want you to put a banner across the sound, with the words, "Welcome to Montana" across it,' Frank told John and Jim. He wanted cables going from the top of a hill on one side of the sound to cables attached to the top of a hill on the other side; a span of at least a couple of kilometres. He wanted absolutely everyone who came across on the ferry from Wellington to Picton to know with absolute certainty that Montana wasn't in this place: Montana WAS this place. Maps be damned. The boat went back to Picton, and Frank, Jim and John drove back to Blenheim and returned to work.

Of course, the banner never went beyond the idea stage, probably because any sensible person would know that the winds swirling through the Sounds would rip a banner to shreds in seconds, even if anyone ever managed to engineer a way to put one up. But Frank always planned on a grand scale, and never gave a second thought about turning one of our country's natural treasures into an advertisement for himself. I hate to think what he would have dreamed up if he had ever spent time at Milford Sound.

Frank was a guy who understood and wholeheartedly embraced the fact that getting people pissed for a living had made him absolutely drunk with power. It was Mate, however, who showed me the power of wine when you are in a tight spot.

Even when Mate became a millionaire several times over, he didn't get distracted by the toys and trinkets of the rich. He wasn't interested in sports cars or helicopters or a company plane that could get him wherever he wanted to go. He could have afforded to hire a fleet of planes, never mind one to get him around New Zealand. Instead, he loved driving his massive truck, his pride and joy, and would take it all the way down from Auckland to Wellington, drive it onto the ferry and continue on from Picton to Blenheim.

But one time on his return trip, there was no room on the ferry. Mate sent me to the Blenheim railway station, which is where you booked your spot on the ferry back then. I came back to the vineyard and said to him, 'I'm sorry, the boat's full. I can't get you on.'

'Fuck it,' he said. 'Come on.'

We drove back to the railway station, and Mate hopped out, walked around to the back of the truck, and pulled out a case of wine. He stomped inside, right past the queue and up to the station manager's desk. Mate let the case drop with a dramatic thud.

'I need to get on this boat,' he said calmly.

'Yep, okay, done,' the manager said, grabbing the case.

A case of wine, I discovered that day, is the greatest form of currency. It is something, I have since learned, several times over, that can get you out of any jam, almost anywhere in the world.

CHAPTER 5

SLAPSTICK
VITICULTURE

TO MANY, WINE IS A RELIGION. AND I HAVE HEARD
it said that 'where religion begins, all logic and reason end', which pretty much convinces me that wine is, indeed, a religion. It must be, since that's the only explanation for how nonsensical nearly every aspect of Montana's first few years in Marlborough were. Although the company's arrival is widely believed to be the event horizon that ensured that the modern New Zealand wine industry would survive and thrive, that's not really the case. Virtually nothing went according to plan because, well, there simply wasn't one. We were all cast members in the viticultural equivalent of an episode of *Fawlty Towers*.

For starters, very few of the cuttings we planted actually grew and matured into vines, simply because they had no roots. Pluck a branch off a tree, stick it in the ground somewhere else and see how well it grows; that's essentially what we were doing with grapevines.

Now, just take a moment to imagine the sense of despair we all felt (from us lowly workers up to the vineyard managers), gazing at an expanse

Jim Hamilton surveying the Brancott vineyard from 'Rob's Nob', now the site of the Brancott Heritage Restaurant (Fairfax Media NZ/*Marlborough Express*)

of decrepit dust marked with only the occasional sign of life. All of those weeks of backbreaking work, planting vine after vine, for virtually nothing. Granted, we were all partly to blame, since we had planted a significant percentage of the cuttings upside down.

None of us working on the planting line had had a lick of experience or training, yet we had each been handed a bucket full of cuttings and told to plant one at the mark along the cable, then move to the next row. Most of us wouldn't have known how to look at the cutting and determine which end of it was the top; most of us had never even seen a grapevine before. And there wasn't exactly an arrow painted on each one, or a tag reading 'This way up.'

This truckload of vine cuttings was badly damaged by frost en route from Auckland. (Fairfax Media NZ/*Marlborough Express*)

If you look at the buds on a cutting, they should be pointing in one direction or the other: the direction they are pointing in is usually towards the top. But Nature is a fickle beast, so not all cuttings look alike. If the buds are growing straight out, the untrained eye wouldn't be able to detect which end is which on the cutting.

Over the years I have heard all sorts of percentages thrown about as to the number of cuttings that were planted upside down in those first Marlborough vineyards: some say it was half, some say one-third, some say one-tenth, some say none. I don't think anyone will ever know, and it's not as if it even matters, because the strike rate in all three of the first Montana vineyards was, at most, 30 per cent. In other words, more than two of every three cuttings we planted wound up dead.

Even if the cuttings had roots, the number that would have grown into vines wouldn't have been much greater, for the simple reason that Marlborough is essentially a desert, and 1973 was one of the driest years on record. With no

Ken Dawson and Phil Sutherland placing cardboard cones over the cuttings
(Fairfax Media NZ/*Marlborough Express*)

irrigation, abnormally low rainfall and the nor'west winds howling through, a cactus, a camel and a dune beetle would all have struggled to survive.

Before anyone thought of getting water to the new vineyards, though, Wayne Thomas instructed that the vines be protected from the spring frost. Unfortunately, the preventative measure he prescribed to do this has written him into Marlborough lore — where he is fated to become forever known for this one mistake rather than any of the many good decisions he made. Wayne decreed that each newly planted vine must be covered with a cardboard cone. The idea was that the cone would protect the base of the vine from the cold air, especially if dirt was mounded up around the base of each cone. It all seems intelligent and innocent enough, until you consider that there were three-quarters of a *million* newly planted vines. Covering them all would require weeks, and no measure taken to secure the cones in place would be a match for Marlborough's mighty winds.

Eventually, many thousands of cones covered the newly planted vines.
(Fairfax Media NZ/*Marlborough Express*)

No one who lived in Blenheim or Renwick around that time could possibly forget the oversized confetti flying around the valley as if the region were a surprise party for Brobdingnagians. The cardboard cones were everywhere, piled up on residents' lawns, cluttering sheep paddocks, and tumbling along every road. The beneficial upshot was that local residents scooped the cones up by the armload, realising that they would be quite useful on the tomato plants in their gardens. But for Montana it was just money down the drain and, worse, the cones that actually did remain affixed to the cuttings made those vines colder by trapping the frosty air. The cones also blocked the sunlight, making it all the more difficult for the vines to grow.

In Wayne's defence, a spring frost is something all growers and wineries worry about today, as such a weather event can burn off the vines' newly formed buds and set back the season by several weeks or months. Essentially it forced the vine to grow new buds and start over, leaving it with only a

Jim Hamilton checking a new planting (Fairfax Media NZ/*Marlborough Express*)

small chance to grow and ripen grapes by autumn. Marlborough's most famous spring-frost disaster came in 2003, wiping out hectare after hectare of budding crops. On new plantings, today, we employ a reusable plastic sleeve that is a much sturdier and more effective version of the cardboard cone. Wayne's head was in the right place, but you know what they say: it's all about execution. And placing the cones on the vines was such dreadful work that those of us who did it were more entertained and relieved than dismayed at the sight of cardboard cluttering the roadways. (Even though we had to make our way back through the vineyard, day after day, replacing all of the cones that had blown away.)

Not only was the scale of the work daunting, but we came up with a mind-numbingly boring system in which two people would sit on the back of a trailer that was being pulled along each row by a tractor. One person would hand the cardboard cone to the other, who would position it, and a third person walking behind and carrying a hoe would mound the dirt around the base of the vine. The work was so dull that we created little rituals to keep ourselves focused and entertained. For example, if you missed a vine or you went too slowly, the driver would stop, join the other two guys, and hold you down while you got a couple of pumps up your shirt with the grease can. This, I can say from experience, is incredibly unpleasant.

Nearly as maddening was the method conceived for watering the vines, since irrigation was deemed unnecessary early on. Even though the solution we came up with was a bit Heath Robinson, it probably saved a decent number of the vines from dying in that first year. Montana brought in four petrol tankers, which were driven down to the Wairau River each day to pump water. Once full, they would drive to Brancott and fill 500-litre fibreglass tanks, which were placed on trailers and hitched to tractors. Two workers would sit on the back of the trailer as it was pulled along the rows, and each person had a pedal and a hose connected to the tank. Upon pressing the pedal with their foot, a litre of water would flush out of the hose and onto each vine. It wasn't perfect, but it was better than nothing ... most of the time.

One problem was that the water and dirt often just rushed out of the bottom of each cardboard cone. The other issue was that we had planted slightly more mature vines — grown at a nursery Wayne was running in Auckland — in place of the cuttings that had died, and when the water flowed onto these new, young plants, their cardboard cones would fill up with the dirt and water, essentially drowning them.

After a while it began to seem that, if Nature couldn't find a way to kill each vine, then we certainly could.

Another unfortunate lesson we learned the hard way was that cheaper is not necessarily better. To get the vines to grow straight up, a plan was devised to plant a stake beside each one. Shiploads of wooden stakes were brought from Malaysia to Picton, bags and bags of them piled in heaps at the port — and they were bloody useless. The trees from which they were sourced all had a disease called brittle heart, which is basically rot in the core of the wood. So every time you tried to push one of the stakes into the hard, dry dirt, it would shatter into tiny pieces.

We had similar problems driving posts into the ground. The dirt was so hard and dry that many of the posts would just snap as the driver hit them from the top — especially if they were placed above a large rock beneath the surface. This was often the case, as the ground was initially not cultivated deeply enough. Even on a good day now, posting remains a brutal job for the crew: usually two guys walk alongside a tractor, which pulls the post-driver. It was worse back then, though, as the posts were covered in splinters, which were just hell on your hands.

But one member of our crew had an even bigger problem. He was a nice, quiet guy who lived in a commune. He ate only vegetables, never any rubbish, but one day he started getting really sick and began to go downhill ever so quickly. He lost weight and his hair started falling out, but test after test revealed nothing wrong with him, until one last doctor ordered a blood screening — on a hunch — and wound up saving his life. It turned out that this bloke had been grabbing a splinter off each post as he was setting them

in the ground, and chewing on it like it was a toothpick. He had no idea —
and nor did we — that the posts were treated with an array of chemicals,
arsenic chief among them. With each splinter he chewed, he was slowly
poisoning himself to death!

Not to sound heartless, but if he had kicked the bucket some of us might
have envied him a bit, considering the seeming lack of sanity behind the
orders we tended to receive. While the intentions were always sincere, an
ill-informed experimental approach to one simple problem typically led to
a host of ensuing bad decisions.

For example, if you look at a vineyard today, you will see perfectly strung,
tight wires along each row, the most important stationary one about waist-
high. This gives each vine something to cling to, and allows it to remain in
a sturdy, straight position that is easy to manage throughout the season,
especially at harvest time. But back in 1973, no one could figure out how
to keep the wire attached to each post; the staples popped out almost
immediately. So Wayne Thomas decided that the wire should be looser and
crimped, to help each vine grow upwards more naturally.

Thankfully, this never got past the idea phase, because each vine would
have grown more or less how it wanted to, and collectively the vines would
have popped the wire off the posts. Fortunately, at least a little bit of logic
eventually prevailed. We were able to affix a perfectly straight wire, and,
what's more, we figured out that if you tied a string from the wire to the top
of the vine, the vine would follow this string and grow straight up. Simple.
The more we over-thought things, we came to realise, the more we would
screw them up.

Despite the onslaught of Sisyphean tasks, I started to become interested
in the work. For the first time in my life, I remember thinking that this was
more than just a job — something I could never say for shearing, driving a
truck, or helping Cathy's dad with stock. Even as screwy or tedious as every
decision felt, I started to believe that I was part of something bigger — and
this was largely due to the efforts of Jim Hamilton.

Me with foreman Lloyd McKay at Fairhall vineyard, 1976,
where we were experimenting with spur pruning

Cathy likes to joke that every Friday when I came home from work I would have been given a new title or promotion of some sort, which is true to some degree, although part of that was simply due to staff attrition. But Jim, I suppose, saw something in me that he didn't see in the other workers. It might have been just that I was always asking questions about the work we were doing. I don't think I ever took on a task without first asking about the desired outcome. I'm quite grateful that, in lieu of just giving me the answers, Jim would lend me books on agriculture or viticulture, or suggest titles to look for or buy (the key one being *General Viticulture* by A.J. Winkler, James A. Cook, W.M. Kliewer and Lloyd A. Lider, which took months to arrive by mail order). In doing so, he helped me understand that, especially with grape-growing, there is often more than one answer to each question. The grape variety, the weather conditions or even the as-yet undetermined could make a difference.

What's more, Jim became a 24/7 resource of sorts. He and his family had moved into a house on the Fairhall vineyard, near Blenheim's golf course. Whenever I had a question or a concern, I could always solicit his advice. That usually resulted in yet another book to read, but I didn't mind. Jim is a modest guy, and will always say that he identified me as one of the more useful workers since I had experience with growing plants. But I got the sense that Jim knew he had rekindled something in me, which was the hunger for knowledge that my mother had instilled in me so long ago. I reckon I was also inspired by the birth of our first daughter, Victoria, in 1974. Nothing motivates a person professionally like the arrival of a child, which is why it is probably true that children and career advancement seem to coincide for so many.

I was promoted to manager of the Fairhall vineyard, Dick Simpson became manager at Brancott, and Clive Drummond ran Renwick, with Jim supervising the three of us, and John Marris handling the administrative side of Montana's Marlborough operation. The managers would meet every week to talk about the small and large tasks at hand, then execute them with our respective crews.

Even so, it was still an era of uncertainty. As much as the work just kept coming and coming — there was always something new to do or to figure out — we were all somewhat nervous that this party wasn't going to last, as if this was just one big, goofy experiment on which Montana might pull the plug at any moment. We had ample distraction from what felt like the inevitable: from planting and managing cover crops to setting up a Marlborough-based nursery. (The nursery kept going, 24/7, all year long, getting vines ready to take the place of any cuttings that didn't grow.) *But why keep the charade going?*, we couldn't help but wonder, as in those first couple of years we wouldn't manage to grow a single grape. (I didn't know it at the time, but we were so far from producing a viable crop that, at one point, Montana and Seagram were actually very close to calling it quits in Marlborough. John Marris flew to Auckland and was able to buy us another year from

TOP: Potted vines in a glasshouse
ABOVE: Vines being hardened off
under a shade house

Montana. Rumour has it that he saved us all in that meeting, begging the bosses to give Marlborough just one more chance.)

Today I am convinced that one of the reasons Montana didn't tuck its tail and run back to Auckland had to do with visits from experts brought in by its investor, Seagram. The experts could plainly see that, while we were still crawling along, we had a good chance of one day learning to walk. The experts were Agustin Huneeus and Ricardo Vial, both of whom gave their heart and soul to us. They, too, had at one time struggled to make vineyards produce in their respective homelands of California and Chile, but they had had nobody to whom they could turn. They failed at experiment after experiment until they found techniques that worked, so both gents were wholly empathetic and eager to see us succeed without spending as many years turning down as many dead ends as they once had. Agustin is known as a pioneer for his winery Quintessa, world-renowned today as one of Napa's best. (The US$120 you would spend on a bottle of the winery's Cabernet-based red blend will all but assure you of this.) A board member of Montana, representing Seagram's interest, he arrived in Marlborough in about 1975, and was quick to point out that our biggest problem was irrigation — which we already knew. But he was also the first to offer a viable solution on what could be done with the plants of varying ages scattered throughout each vineyard.

Since only a small percentage of the cuttings we had initially planted had matured into full vines, the cuttings that died had been replaced the following year with plants that had been grown in one of the nurseries. And we did the same the year after that, so in each vineyard there were big, two-year-old vines next to one-year-old plants next to new plantings only a few weeks or months old. Agustin showed us that we needn't continue chasing our tails, replacing vine after vine across hectare after hectare. Instead, where there was a gap in the canopy we could take a long shoot off one of the nearby mature vines, train it to grow off to the side, and, after a year, cut it off and use that as a replacement vine. This sort of thing works much better in a warmer climate such as the Napa Valley (Agustin and other experts, at the time, believed Marlborough was best suited to grow Cabernet Sauvignon), but it was just one of several ideas Agustin brought, along with unrelenting encouragement — something we didn't get much of from the Montana brass as time went on and results failed to materialise.

Not far behind Agustin was his cousin, Ricardo Vial, vineyard manager for Viña Concha y Toro in Chile, who was also encouraged by our progress. While he, too, brought a range of successful techniques from his native land, he also helped us understand what we already knew: that in the vineyards there is no such thing as the industry standard. In each and every wine-producing region around the world, the dirt and the climate are unique; the only way to grow grapes successfully is to continue experimenting and innovating in your own time and place until you find what works.

Indeed, we started to see promising signs after a few years, for two reasons. The first was that we got the propagation programme going properly in a Marlborough-based nursery, eventually mastering a system in which we could grow vine after vine with incredible efficiency; the second was that the dry, dusty conditions of 1973 gave way to several years of much more even, mild conditions in which grapevines could grow comfortably. We experienced the right balance of sun and rainfall, but, more importantly, the killer spring frosts everyone worried about never materialised. When they did strike, they were powerful enough to kill the tomato plants in people's gardens, but they weren't beastly enough to harm the vines, which have evolved to withstand harsh conditions in most parts of the world. That's why grapevines can survive for decades; in parts of France, Australia, Spain and California, there are vines that are more than a century old.

We became comfortable enough with our work in the vineyards and in the nursery that Cathy and I uprooted all of the vegetables and trees we had been growing on the land around our house and planted every square centimetre with Müller-Thurgau vines. We were among the first contract growers for Montana, as was John Marris. Joining us were Phil and Chris Rose, who would later found Wairau River; Neil and Judy Ibbotson, who would launch Saint Clair; and a handful of others who still grow grapes or make wine in Marlborough today.

I wish I could say that everything was easy from that point forward, and that Marlborough's path to worldwide recognition was thereafter clear. But in 1976 Jim left Montana and Marlborough, so I didn't have a mentor after that, much less an advocate. He told me years later that he recommended me to take over his position upon his departure, but that Montana rejected the idea. God only knows if management actually gave it any consideration, as around that time they were busy spending so much of their intellectual and financial capital on disassembling a winery on the North Island and shipping it down, bit by bit, for reassembly in Marlborough. It was Montana's very own London Bridge, and any time I and my crew didn't spend in the vineyard we were tightening bolts on that Frankenstein of a winery.

I continued managing the Fairhall vineyard up to and through most of 1979 — more or less taking direction as it came, hoping for the best in the field and with my family at home. I was pretty much left to my own devices, as John Marris was usually busy inspecting or buying new properties, as

We welcomed renowned wine writer — and acclaimed opera singer —
Charles Metcalfe during one of his visits to Marlborough.

well as selling others that were deemed either too wet or too dry. There
were crews cultivating land, and others building tractor sheds or handling
general maintenance. Montana almost felt like an Orwellian commune,
with everyone just doing their thing, and not really striving to learn more
or expand skill sets and knowledge beyond their areas of immediate focus.
Everything seemed to work well enough and seemed to be — finally —
running smoothly. But mental stimulation was suddenly in short supply.

Around the time that Victoria started to walk and talk, I began to feel
there was nothing left for me to do at Montana, even though I was constantly
running at lightning speed. I was doing everything asked of me, yet absorbing
and learning nothing — even if, towards the last couple of years of my tenure,
we were growing grapes in Marlborough and producing wine, ultimately
helping the Yukich brothers' long-odds gamble start to pay off. But I knew
it was time to leave — if only I could find the right place to give my mind
the kind of exercise that my body experienced every day among the vines.

I DIGRESS ...

One of the most attractive aspects of working in the wine industry is that you are often afforded the opportunity to visit far-flung destinations around the world — and establish and maintain lifelong connections to some wonderful people you never would have encountered otherwise. I couldn't have possibly imagined that, less than a decade after I first showed up for work at the Brancott vineyard in 1973, I would start to fill my passport courtesy of invitations to places that I could have reasonably expected only ever to know as coloured blobs on a globe, nothing more.

That's one of the things that draws so many young, intelligent, adventurous and innovative souls to Marlborough every fall to work in our wineries and vineyards at harvest time. Some work as many as four or five harvests in a year, starting in Australia in February. They then move on to New Zealand for March and April, before making a mad dash to Argentina or Chile to work there in May and June; then they head north to the west coast of the United States or Europe to work from August or so right through October. Such a lifestyle was unheard of in the 1970s and 1980s, and even so I probably lacked the requisite youthful spirit to do that sort of thing myself. My travels mainly involve entertaining distributors or importers, or doing a song-and-dance routine several times each day for restaurants and retailers in a foreign market. Sometimes it can be a bit silly, such as a visit to an Atlanta supermarket I made in the late 1990s. It turned out that no one had bothered to tell me in advance that Georgia state law at the time prohibited in-store tastings. This particular store's wine buyer was paranoid about violating the law, so she suggested we open a bottle in the womens' toilet and sip the wine in there, where no one would see us. For the rest of the day I had to walk up to customers wandering the aisles, introduce myself and simply ask them if they would like to buy a bottle of my wine (some of them were brave enough, despite the awkwardness).

Although I enjoy travelling and talking about our wines with everyday consumers, that part isn't as much fun, in my opinion, as the continuing education I might receive by attending seminars or trade shows, or informally exchanging ideas with viticulturists and winemakers who are experimenting and innovating in their own environs. Often, they come to Marlborough, usually bringing along with them new and interesting wines from their countries, or bottles they have discovered on their travels. More of these opportunities presented themselves after Marlborough saw the arrival of Daniel Le Brun in the early 1980s, when he established Cellier Le Brun. (Today, he owns and operates No. 1 Family Estate, unquestionably the best producer of sparkling wines in the Southern Hemisphere.)

Daniel had spent most of his life in the vineyards of Champagne, just as his father had, and his grandfather and so on for several generations. But Daniel was eager to venture out on his own — and he believed he had found the perfect cool, dry, sunny climate where he could grow Pinot Noir and Chardonnay to craft sparkling wines as good as, or better than, the ones his family and peers had spent centuries making in his homeland. Some locals called Daniel 'the mad Frenchman' — but only those who didn't understand or appreciate his experience, knowledge and ambition.

Daniel and I took an instant liking to each other, and our wives got on well with each other too. He brought much personal and professional enjoyment to me and to Marlborough, but he is rarely acknowledged for two other contributions to our industry. The most obvious one is the first real hint of international credibility; the second is that he opened a connection to European experience and knowledge where little to none previously existed. Only a few short years after Daniel put his claimstake in the ground, European invitations and opportunities for Kiwi growers and winemakers began to present themselves more frequently.

Over the years, Daniel and I have made multiple trips to Europe together. One two-week excursion in the 1980s took us through several vineyards and regions of France, ending in Montpellier. As we had a little extra time at the end, we decided that it would be fun to drive up through the Alps, across into Italy, and depart Europe from Milan. Unfortunately, we hadn't counted on being able to hire only a shitty, tiny little A-class Mercedes — nor had we counted on there being a massive snowstorm.

Everything came to a screaming halt at the Fréjus Road Tunnel (which connects France and Italy), resulting in a long, snaking traffic jam stretching for kilometres. Fortunately, we were near the front of it, but we still sat there in the car for a while, just trying to keep warm and discussing when we might get through the bottleneck. Daniel then uttered the last words you want to hear in such a situation: 'I think I need to have a crap.'

This being Europe (and the highway, no less), there wasn't a loo for kilometres in any direction. So Daniel did his best not to draw any attention to himself as he stepped out of the car and off the bank, into the snow to pop a squat. It must have been as cold and uncomfortable as it was embarrassing, so I decided to take the opportunity to walk to the other side of the road for a quick pee. Others were doing the same, as well as milling about between cars, smoking cigarettes and chatting to pass the time.

We both returned to the car at about the same time, and from outside the rental car I could see just how tiny it was — and how much space there was between the queues of cars and trucks in each lane.

'You know what?' I said to Daniel. 'I reckon if you drive and I push, this little car will squeeze right through the middle of all these cars. The pass is only a mile up — I think we can make it.'

If you think European drivers are mental on a good day, you should see how irate they get when a couple of wacky foreigners in a shitty little rental car start squeezing their way through traffic, unwilling to wait their turn. Horns blared and foreign-tongued insults filled our ears for the entire kilometre or so that we pushed through the snow and sleet, with mere millimetres of available space either side of our car. But we just carried on, navigating our way through the cars, trucks and buses until we got to the last little stretch near the top of the pass.

When we got to the top, we found that a big bank of snow had been created by a plough, and it was this that was causing the backup: there was no way through. We thought we might be able to dig through it with our hands, but, before we could try, a lunatic in a Peugeot came out of nowhere and smashed into the snowbank, absolutely rooting the front of his car. We had to thank him, though, since he loosened the snowbank enough that we were able to dig the Peugeot out, banged up as it was, then create a wide enough gap to push our hire car through.

We continued on our journey, down to the village on the other side, on to Milan and back home. We would later learn that our car was one of the few to make it through: almost everyone else remained stuck in that traffic jam for two or three days, and it was one of the worst Europe had ever experienced.

Sometimes it takes a couple of guys who have spent their whole lives in tight, orderly rows to see a solution in so desperate a situation. Well, that, and more than one innovation has occurred to someone as they sat on the crapper.

CHAPTER 6

CLIMBING THE CORPORATE LADDER

BY 1979, I NEEDED A BREAK. BOTH CATHY AND I were exhausted, but for me it was as much mental as physical. After a long day of chasing my own tail around the Fairhall vineyard, I would chase Victoria around the house at night. She had boundless energy as a child, and still has plenty to burn today, even with two children of her own (both now teenagers), as well as a full-time job running marketing at our winery. Cathy was nursing all day at the hospital, then she would work at an office in town at night, making good extra money transferring old, handwritten motor registrations into a somewhat rudimentary form of computerisation. Even though the job was just typing, it seemed somewhat space-age for the time. So after her day job she was able to experience something new and exciting for the era — and get paid for it. But I had no such outlet.

I therefore applied to, and was accepted at, Wagga Wagga Agricultural Institute, now part of Charles Sturt University in New South Wales, which is among the better places in the English-speaking world to earn the highest viticultural and winemaking credentials (the others are the Waite Campus at the University of Adelaide, Lincoln University in Christchurch, and the University of California at Davis.) I decided it was time to beef up my credentials and commit to doing so full-time. Around the time that Vic was born, I had been taking a correspondence course in horticulture, and I was doing quite well with it. But along with Vic's arrival and the million things I had going on between Fairhall and our own 4 hectares of vines surrounding our house, I decided to drop the course even though I was about three-quarters of the way through it.

One of my only regrets in life is that I never picked up the course again, because at that time it was possible to earn a doctorate — I would have been among the first, if not *the* first, Kiwi viticulturist with a PhD. Even though I didn't have a horticultural background or a university education, basic science as well as general botany came to me quite naturally. I learned that if it's something you love, it all just falls into place so easily. I assumed that Montana would see the value in me having a serious academic credential, so I applied for a leave of absence to attend Wagga Wagga.

'Sure!' my superiors said without hesitation. 'You'll be gone, what, two weeks? We can't have you away for any longer than that.'

I didn't bother telling them that earning a degree takes a bit longer, so I decided to drop it and plod back to Fairhall. But soon after, in early 1980, Jim Hamilton made a return visit to Marlborough. Since the time he had left Montana in 1976, he had been working for rival Corbans in its vineyards in Gisborne, in the North Island. We had kept in touch on and off all the while, so I knew a good deal about what he and his company were working on. At least, I thought I did.

'Look,' he said to me not long after he had arrived back in Marlborough, 'it's no secret, but Corbans have just bought 1,000 acres [400 hectares] in Rapaura.'

Apparently, they had been keeping an eye on things, and patiently observing progress as Montana and Seagram absorbed the time and cost of paving the way in Marlborough. One thing you have to remember, though, is

that in 1973 Montana had moved quickly, scooping up land that was not only cheap, but was widely assumed to be marginal if not impossible for growing a crop of any kind. That is why most of Montana's original plantings were spots in the western and southern corners of the valley. A commitment to Rapaura by Corbans, however, was quite the opposite of a quick land-grab.

Rapaura sits northeast of Renwick and hugs the Wairau River: a sunny, fertile, exposed area that includes the lands where Cloudy Bay, Huia, Matua, Herzog, Whitehaven, Wairau River and the Allan Scott winery all sit today. Some of this land was pasture, but much of it was laid to apple and stone-fruit orchards. Corbans wasn't making a gamble in the same way Montana had seven years earlier, taking a brief look and bidding on cheap dirt; this was a big investment in proven ground. In no uncertain terms, Corbans was sending a message to Montana: *You were first, but we are better.*

'We need someone to run it and manage it,' Jim said, with a seeming pride that he was able to offer me the job he had been unable to a few years earlier. 'Interested?'

I didn't hesitate. But as it was already early in 1980, the harvest was just on the horizon. So I stayed with Montana through May, to ensure a smooth transition rather than leave the company in the lurch. And despite all of the difficulties, frustration and general madness of the seven years I spent at Montana, I must admit that the company ultimately did know how to express gratitude. Upon my departure, Montana presented me with an engraved silver platter and two accompanying antique crystal claret jugs. The set is absolutely beautiful, and remains among my most prized possessions (even if I don't polish the pieces as often as I should). For all the Yukich brothers' faults, which were exacerbated by their unbridled ambition, they certainly knew how to say 'thank you'. And in doing so, they reminded me that I had no easy task ahead: that my work ethic and curiosity had got me to where I was, and those were the very things I would need to rely on most in the future. With Corbans moving into Marlborough and others certain to follow, everything was sure to get harder, not easier.

First, though, I had to interview for the job, as Corbans was part of a much larger, more tangled corporate machine than Montana. I was a bit nervous, because I had never actually been interviewed for a job before — ever. I wasn't really sure what to do or say.

I flew up to Auckland on a Sunday to meet with Bob Matthew, who was then head of the New Zealand arm of Rothmans International, a tobacco company which by that time had full control of Corbans. Bob was the master puppeteer at Corbans, pulling all the marionette strings on every character. Much like Montana getting into bed with Seagram, Corbans had got to a point where it had found that, while it was perfectly good at buying land, planting vines, growing grapes and making wine, it was not doing such a great job at selling the wine. The company needed money, and more or less gave up to Rothmans a significant portion of equity in, and control of, the company in order to get more capital. That's one of the rather unfortunate pages in the history of nearly every New Zealand winery, large or small. Montana needed Seagram; Corbans needed a tobacco company (that eventually became public enemy number one due to its corporate headquarters being located in apartheid-era South Africa); Delegat's needed a bailout from the Wilson Neill Corporation (although Delegat's eventually bought back its shares); Villa Maria went into receivership and had to bring in new investors to start over.

I wasn't in Bob's palatial, luxurious office for long. Rather than ask me questions, he delivered a monologue he had probably recited countless times before my butt ever landed in a chair opposite his desk, and as he spoke I realised a couple things. First was that he was clearly a control freak (an attribute I actually admired, as years later I would invite him to serve on the Allan Scott winery's board, which he did for a decade); second, this wasn't so much a job interview as the boss laying down the law about what he expected of me and everyone else under his thumb. Bob repeatedly reminded me that Rothmans had invested millions in Corbans, and that the company expected to see a return sooner rather than later. Yes, Corbans had a great family and business legacy, he told me, but they had fallen behind the times, so it would be important that Jim and I act quickly, clearly and in lockstep on every decision; Bob wanted no hints of drama. But he said one thing in particular that I never forgot: 'Family is important, but the job is equally important.'

I was out of the office in a daze and back on a plane to Blenheim before I realised what had happened. All I could think was: *Shit, this is big-time.*

Corbans had found their fortunes dimming largely because the company only produced and sold cask wines, mostly blends, and they had no presence in bars or restaurants. There was a five-variety red blend, as well as a medium Riesling and a white blend, mostly Müller-Thurgau. It wasn't as if New Zealand's collective tastes were already shifting to dry table wines (although this would start to occur in the early 1980s), but Corbans had remained stuck in neutral in nearly all aspects of the business, for decades. It was clear that several changes would be needed, even if we weren't yet sure what they were. Within months of Corbans' move into Marlborough, Australian wine giant Penfolds extended its tentacles into the region as well. The competition would soon get very hot.

Looking back, what's interesting to me about these three giants' attempts at Marlborough domination is that they all approached the region differently. Montana grabbed whatever land it could buy, as quickly as it could; Corbans kept its eye on a very specific section of the valley for several years and waited for the right moment to pounce, then concentrated its resources on that one area (with modest additional grower support); and Penfolds relied mostly on a large, loose network of growers. Not long into my tenure at Corbans, I created a large, colour-coded map of the region: Montana's vineyards were blue, Corbans' were yellow and Penfolds' were red. In an incredibly short time, my map looked a pixelated mess, and, with growers shifting their contracts between wineries so often, it eventually became impossible to keep up. The real reason I trashed the map, though, was that I realised that it was more important to focus on what Corbans was doing, not everyone else.

Indeed, there was plenty to do. The plan was to plant all of the land as quickly as possible, and leave a spot on the corner of the property for the construction of a winery — which happens to be where Matua's Marlborough winery sits today, at the corner of Jacksons and Rapaura roads. We developed an irrigation scheme that would channel waste water towards the south (into the land that is now occupied by our family winery and its surrounding vineyard, as well as our house across the street, and extends all the way to Cloudy Bay's winery), and we also put windbreaks through the massive, open area so that

Piling debris into fire heaps at the new Corbans vineyard, 1980

we could apply sprays underneath the trees. I was in charge of arranging and executing every aspect of this.

Bookworm that I am, I spent a lot of time looking into the history of this area. Originally, it had been one large farm called Moorland Settlement, but it had been split into several smaller, individual land holdings after World War I. (For the purposes of this book, we will treat the area as two separate, large blocks: Moorland would be the area that today is occupied by our winery and Matua; Settlement was the area behind it to the west, running all the way up to where Wairau River's winery sits today.) Prior to this area becoming vineyard land, after the post–World War I subdivision, some of the land became orchards, some of it became pasture land, and some of it became reasonably productive farmland. Because it had been carved by the Wairau River more recently than the far west and south of the valley, the soil and nutrient quality varied drastically throughout the blocks.

Driving end strainers into the ground, Corbans, 1980

The drier, rockier sections required irrigation; there was no debate, as there had been in the early days at Brancott. So we pulled out all the stops to make sure we got everything right the first time, and Corbans was able to produce its first crop in 1982, just twenty-four months or so after we had started. That's lightning speed, even by today's standards, as newly planted land typically takes about three years to produce a viable crop of grapes.

We had so much Sauvignon Blanc, in fact, that we were selling it off to other wineries, mainly Selaks and Nobilo. While I could tell you that this was the start of the Marlborough Sauvignon Blanc boom, strictly speaking that wouldn't be true. In fact, nobody really knows how or why Sauvignon Blanc became our signature grape, except to say that Marlborough evolved in much the same way as pretty much every other wine region, in that growers start with multiple varieties, then reassess every few years. With each vineyard you start with, say, Sauvignon Blanc, Chenin Blanc, Chardonnay, Gewürztraminer and Riesling. If Chardonnay, Riesling and Sauvignon Blanc seem to grow healthier, bigger crops, you plant more of those varieties and not the others. Then, a few years after that, if Sauvignon and Riesling show more promise than Chardonnay, you plant more of those two varieties. And so on.

While I am not aware of any records that say who planted the first Sauvignon Blanc vines in Marlborough, Clive Drummond recalls planting some in the Renwick vineyard for Montana in 1980. I planted some in a small section of the Fairhall vineyard around the same time, as well, but any number of people were probably a year or two ahead of us. The way Marlborough's story goes, it's a pretty safe bet that Sauvignon Blanc just happened to grow better and produce bigger crop volumes more consistently over time than other varieties, which is why Corbans had so much of it to sell off. But we also had quite a bit of success with Riesling, as well as the Chenin Blanc and Müller-Thurgau that we had asked our growers to plant, so we had yet to identify Sauvignon Blanc as our international superstar. Just as, or more, interesting (to me, anyway) were the advancements and innovations taking place. The industry was experiencing an explosion of inventiveness and opportunity, in fact. Everywhere you looked, it seemed someone was conjuring a solution to a previously unaddressed problem and improving efficiency or quality — especially in the vineyards.

One day, when we were first cultivating the ground at Rapaura, a car pulled over to the side of the road. A wiry guy wearing glasses emerged from it, approached me and asked if we were planting a vineyard. I told him yes, that we were planting 400 hectares.

'I'm building a machine to inject posts into the ground, and I guarantee I'll be half the price of anything else you do,' he said after he had introduced himself as Dick Pike. 'You won't need to buy a post-driver. I'm just building the machine, but can we shake hands on it that you'll give me a go on this job once I finish building it?'

'Shit, that's a long shake,' I said.

'I don't need money, I just want to shake hands on a deal,' he said. *Nothing ventured, nothing gained*, I thought as we interlocked our grips and the fellow disappeared. A few months later, we were ready to start driving posts and, in truth, I had forgotten about the roadside meeting. We had bought a post-driver and begun work when the phone in the office rang.

'I've got it built!' said Dick at the other end of the line. 'Are you ready to go?'

'Uh ...' was all I could muster, and he immediately knew that we had started without him.

Dick Pike's remarkable post driver

'We had a deal,' he said. 'Look, I understand you had to get started, but just let me bring it over from Nelson, and give us a trial. I guarantee you won't be disappointed.'

He arrived at the vineyard the next day with this bizarre-looking contraption on the back of a tractor. True to his word, his machine rammed a perfectly vertical post into the ground every 30 seconds. It was incredible — and it's what everyone used from then on to plant new vineyards.

The most important innovation, however, was the invention of the automatic leaf-plucker. Along with over-cropping (that is, where too many bunches of grapes per vine ultimately dilute the flavour of the wine), one of the biggest impediments to ripening grapes throughout New Zealand vineyards in the 1980s was leaf clutter in the canopy. The denser the canopy, the more it shades the grapes from sunlight, making it harder for them to ripen. Plucking some of the leaves lets in more light and also allows for better airflow, helping to prevent the spread of powdery mildew. We would pull quite a bit of the leaf clutter by hand, but it wasn't efficient, nor are humans terribly consistent with this sort of task along rows and rows and hectares and hectares of vines.

In 1982 Dr Richard Smart, a viticultural consultant from Australia who went on to earn his PhD from Cornell University in New York, was hired by the Ruakura Research Centre to consult to the New Zealand wine industry. He found dense canopies in all of the country's vineyards, and he recommended various approaches — from different pruning methods

Our prototype leaf plucker based on a harvester leaf-extractor fan

to ways in which we could measure the number of leaves and calculate a formula for removing just the right number of them per vine. But then he started to look at a mechanical method of leaf removal with the help of Gallagher Machinery, which was based in Hamilton, near Ruakura's office. Unfortunately, all of the early prototypes were as complicated as they were hideous.

At Corbans, we used an UpRight grape harvester, which had a fan device inside it that removed the leaves from the picked grapes. I remember looking at a tractor and thinking, *I wonder if we can mount the same kind of fan on there? If it sucks air with just the right amount of power, it'll pull the leaves away and cut them off, leaving the grapes undamaged and exposed to air and sunlight. We'd just need a hydraulic arm to raise and lower the fan to match the height of the vines ...*

At the time, Corbans worked with a local machinery supplier called Anderson Collett, which employed a very clever engineer and mechanic named Brent Balcombe. I explained to Brent what I wanted to do, and he was enthusiastic in a way that only a true mechanical nerd can be — and

141

Wolf Blass founder Wolfgang Blass, Corbans general manager Paul Treacher, and me at the launch of a joint Corbans–Wolf Blass venture

we built a prototype that was fast, efficient and worked perfectly. Everyone copied it from then on, including Gallagher Machinery, which produced its own version and took credit for the invention. Up until Brent's death a few years ago from cancer, we would often joke about what an opportunity we had missed in not cashing in on the idea ourselves.

Perhaps most importantly, though, the success we were realising in growing quality grapes afforded me two things. The first was to travel to Adelaide a few times each year to exchange information and ideas with the viticultural team at Wolf Blass, one of the biggest names in Australian wine, which had entered into a trans-Tasman partnership with Corbans. (This included a Wolf Blass–branded Marlborough Sauvignon Blanc, but it didn't sell particularly well. On the bright side, one benefit of the partnership, however, was that I became acquainted with Wolf himself, and he once visited our house when he was in Marlborough. He was upstairs getting showered and changed, and, when he came down the stairs dressed with his trademark bow tie, Josh and Sara — both little kids at the time — screamed in excitement. But only because they believed he was Ronnie Corbett.) The second benefit was that I had free rein and authority to conduct trials and research in the vineyards, which no one else in Marlborough was doing around this time.

An Australasian chemical company that subcontracted for larger conglomerates such as Dow and BASF was always looking for farmers to conduct trials on agrochemicals such as weedkillers or powdery mildew preventatives. Bringing weeds under control is actually the thing that most vineyard managers and viticulturists — although they hate to admit it — spend more time and effort doing than actually growing grapes. Doing agrochemical trials on top of that requires a certain level of pedantry and patience that few possess. I have no idea if this is something to be proud of, but I rather enjoyed the opportunity to partake in and assist the type of botanical research that, to most, is about as exciting as watching paint dry. The chemical companies couldn't take guesses before ramping up production and product rollout, so they relied on people like me to make accurate applications — to the millilitre — of chemicals onto certain vines, rows or blocks, and then record and report the results along with all pertinent weather data. Unless all of the data is perfect, the researchers in charge of each chemical or group of chemicals cannot be certain what is safe for people and the environment before committing to large-scale production, never mind distribution and sales to farmers and vineyard managers like me.

No chemical, however, would be effective in 1982, when the New Zealand wine industry was hit with a massive headwind: phylloxera. This is a microscopic insect that feeds rather happily on the roots of grapevines, and the bugs multiply and spread with incredible ease and speed across vineyards and entire regions. All it takes to spread phylloxera is to drive a tractor through the rows of an infested vineyard, then drive that tractor

to a clean vineyard. (I hate to say it, but we at Corbans were possibly responsible for outbreaks at a couple of vineyards, as we did contracting work on several growers' properties and it's likely we didn't hose down the tractors sufficiently as we drove them from vineyard to vineyard.) Similarly, if workers walk among the rows of an infested vineyard in the morning and then a clean vineyard in the afternoon, the bugs can hitch a ride on the workers' shoes.

The effects of phylloxera are hard to see at first, but over a couple of seasons you notice that, while the vines look healthy from a distance, growing a perfectly green leaf canopy, they are not producing any grapes. With the roots of each vine, well, rooted, the plant can't take up the water and nutrients it needs to proliferate, which a vine does by growing grapes. (From a bio-evolutionary standpoint, a vine grows tasty grapes so that an animal will come along and eat them, then shit out the seeds somewhere else for new vines to grow.) No healthy roots means no grapes — and no wine.

Most of Corbans' vineyards were in Gisborne, which was hit especially hard by phylloxera. Nowadays, if you are planting a vineyard you graft your cuttings of, say, Sauvignon Blanc onto the rootstocks of any one of several varieties of native North American vines that are resistant to phylloxera, and you will have no problem. There are hardly any vines in New Zealand today that are not grafted. The real issue with phylloxera, however, is the psychological effect it has on grape growers; it's rather like herpes, in that it spreads faster because no one wants to admit they have it. As a result they carry on for far too long as if nothing is wrong. Ultimately, growers incur greater cost by not simply addressing the problem immediately and replanting on the resistant rootstock.

Corbans had invested heavily in Gisborne, and was struggling to find solutions to several problems, phylloxera among them, but also climatic diseases such as mildew. However, Corbans' Auckland-based winemaker, Norbert Seibel, was a German, and he did his best to maintain his professional contacts back home. Kevin Peterson, the general manager of Corbans at the time, suggested in 1982 that I ask Norbert to help me plan a trip to Germany and Switzerland to see how the viticultural research institutes and nurseries there approached grafting and a range of the other issues that were dogging us at the time. This also presented me with an opportunity to visit chemical companies in Europe, primarily BASF, for whom I had been conducting all those trials.

Coincidentally, only a couple months before I was scheduled to depart for Europe, a strange-looking quartet with foreign accents stepped out of their car at the edge of the Rapaura vineyard. Visitors didn't wander among the rows very often, but I did my best to be pleasant, even though I didn't know who they were or what they were doing there. They told me they were working on emigrating to New Zealand, and were just having a look around.

'Where are you from?' I asked.

'Germany,' said the taller, stockier bloke.

'Ah, I'm headed there soon to visit some contacts in Mosel and the Rheingau,' I said.

'Vee are from Neustadt,' the man said. 'Ees not very far. You must come visit.'

I introduced myself as the fellow scribbled down his contact details on a scrap of paper and handed it to me.

'I am Alex, Alex Giesen,' he said.

During the course of a day you are likely to meet many different types of people — some movers and shakers, some enthusiasts, some mere tyre kickers. I probably placed the Giesens in the last category, as I assumed them to be a family holidaying, not prospecting. I had no idea back then that I was shaking hands with a man who would, in just a few weeks' time, shuttle me around the German countryside — much less that the entire family would migrate to New Zealand and create one of the country's largest and most successful wineries.

It was a difficult time for me to leave for Europe for a few weeks, especially as our second child, Josh, was less than a year old. Just as my career had hit a turning point around the time that Vic had been born, so, too, had it reached another — the move to Corbans — at the time of Josh's arrival in 1981. And now we were expecting Sara at any moment. But there was a sudden belief among the bosses that I was the guy to figure out how the experienced wine-growing world did things — and bring that knowledge back home.

As the trip was sorted relatively quickly, I travelled all the way to London in cattle class, which was far less glamorous in the 1980s than it is today. I wandered in a jet-lagged haze to the train that shuttles weary travellers into the city, then managed to find my hotel in central London, even though it still felt far from anywhere. London seemed absolutely colossal.

In my room, I had a soak in the bath — something I hadn't taken the time to do in years. I then went down to the hotel restaurant and did the most English of things, which was to eat a cucumber sandwich. I went back upstairs, slept like a mummy, then took the train back to the airport to fly to Zurich. As this was long before the advent of email and text messages, I had no clue what I was to do upon arrival other than find my way to the train station, buy a ticket for the two-hour ride to my first meeting point, at Schaffhausen in Switzerland, and rely on the universal language of point-and-grunt should I encounter any confusion. Beyond that, all I had was a name of a contact and a general idea of where I was to meet him.

Of course, I was completely clueless on arrival at Schaffhausen. I was in my early thirties, and I had never been further from home than Australia, never mind to a country whose residents did not speak English as their first language — and this was long before it became so common for Kiwis to travel so far from home. About all I knew was that I was directly north of Zurich,

TOP: A proud father with Joshua, March 1981
ABOVE: Josh with my father, Ben Scott, in 1982

near the German border, and that they made watches here. As I sat at the station's cafeteria, a woman who spoke a bit of broken English did her best to explain to me that all visitors to Schaffhausen tend to meet their hosts near the train station's massive clock. After I had waited there for about half an hour, two fellows sauntered in my direction, one of whom asked me whether I was Mr Scott. We hopped into an Opel car and drove to a small village called Hallau, where I was told I would be taken to the first nursery I was scheduled to visit.

Hallau was a spectacularly beautiful village on the side of a hill, alight in the colours of autumn. I checked myself into a little pub hotel and collapsed onto the big pine bed, complete with feather duvet. I had never seen one before, and all I could think was, *Shit, we do this all wrong at home — this is the most comfortable thing I've ever felt in my life.* But what I really loved about the hotel was that there were long, communal tables where you sat for meals. There were no menus, you were simply brought food, and other guests did their best

to engage you in conversation, even
though they never seemed to go
much further than 'Ows-tra-lee-a?
No? Noi See-land. Ah hah!'

The next morning I was taken to
the nursery, and saw immediately that
these guys were light-years ahead of
us. All of the grapevine material was
coming in from Hungary, all labelled
with metal tags. A crew of workers
would take each bundle of cuttings,
then place it in a big bath of water to
soak for twenty-four hours. The next
day, the bundles would be weighed to
determine whether the cuttings had
gained the requisite 10 per cent in
weight or required more soak time.
The grafters, mostly French, were
incredibly quick, making all of their
cuts with surgical precision and then
connecting the cuttings to the roots
with wax, without using tape, which
we still use in New Zealand today.
They could work by feel, matching

A vineyard in Hallau, Switzerland

the scion and stock without even looking and thereby processing a daunting
1,000 cuttings per *hour*. Everything was then boxed and sent off to a big
glasshouse up the road for planting in pots. Ultimately, I spent two days there,
just watching, taking notes and snapping photographs. The language barrier
made it difficult to ask questions, but the more I watched, the more I learned.

Next, I was driven a few hours past the German border to Freiburg
University, where I was to meet Dr Norbert Becker, a viticulturist who is

ABOVE, LEFT AND RIGHT: Preparing the nursery at Corbans

still considered among the field's most prominent pioneers. (He died in 2012.) First, I went to the office to ask whether Dr Becker was ready to meet with me, but I was told that he was busy teaching a class — although I was welcome to sit in. I crept in through the side door of a large lecture hall, and Dr Becker quickly brought the normal proceedings to a halt and said to the class, 'I like to introduce you all to Meester Schcott, who is here from Noi See-land. Please velcome him.'

The subject of the lecture was powdery mildew, and there were three glasses of wine on the table in front of Dr Becker. At the time he was trying to breed vines that were resistant to the fungus, yet still viable for growing wine grapes.

'Meester Schcott, perhaps you like to taste zee vines?' said Dr Becker.

I had no idea what they were, and I don't suppose anyone else in the room did, either. I tasted the first, and it was obviously Riesling. (By the time this journey had come about, Cathy and I had taken advantage of the Corbans wine allowance granted to senior employees, and we had started to develop a better taste for, and understanding of, wine.) The next two wines were pretty bland and horrible, but I guessed that they were both Chasselas — a relatively useless white variety that's mostly grown in Switzerland and Turkey.

'Ah, Meester Schcott!' Dr Becker said excitedly. 'Vee call it Gutedel, you call it Chasselas. Very vell done, you ver 100 per cent! Class, this is zee only person who has *ever* guessed all three vines correct.'

It was the best guess of all time, although I like to think that Dr Becker took me more seriously as a result. He even insisted that I stay at his house rather than at the hotel. Each night we stayed up until all hours eating, drinking and discussing our work. After a while, I finally told him that it was okay to call me Allan, not Mr Scott.

'Meester Schcott,' he replied, 'vee only exchange our first names with our very, very bischt friends.'

I was sad to leave Dr Becker behind, as I had learned more and more with each minute that passed in his presence. He, perhaps more than anyone else, helped me reach a particularly important conclusion that I typed in my notes at the time. They're words similar to those nearly every New Zealand wine producer lives by today: 'We should [pay] more attention to individual vine tending to allow more healthy vines to produce the inevitable better-quality end product.'

After I bade farewell to Dr Becker, I was scheduled to visit the horticultural headquarters of BASF in Ludwigshafen to discuss some of the trials I had been conducting. All of a sudden I was around legions of scientists in white lab coats. Intimidated as I was at first, it turned out that they were all quite impressed with the progress I had described and the data I had accumulated in Corbans' vineyards. That was a nice validation of the sort I rarely, if ever, received back home — possibly because, as isolated as New Zealand is, we never really knew whether or not we were on the right track. Now I believed I could report back home with confidence that we were. Sadly, though, I remember BASF more for the final night I spent in town, and less so for the work I had conducted for the company.

I was introduced to a fellow Kiwi who handled logistics for a company in New Zealand, but often spent weeks or months at a time working in Germany. He picked me up for dinner, and we drove into Mannheim, the larger, more metropolitan area across the river from Ludwigshafen.

Normally, when you are just getting acquainted with somebody, you don't expect that their first suggestion will be to visit the town's red-light district. But to each his own, so I agreed and we began wandering through the small, sleazy neighbourhood. There was a US military base in Mannheim, so there were a lot of personnel milling about quite contentedly. We had wandered only a few metres down the street where the girls sit in their windows before the guy said to me, 'I think I might go have a session.'

'Not my cup of tea,' I replied, 'but if you want to, go ahead and I'll wait.'

The first woman he approached actually turned him down.

Business must be booming, I thought to myself.

The next one let him inside, and I just sort of stood there, taking in the surroundings for about ten or fifteen minutes. It was sensory overload: women waving and beckoning, men coming and going as if it was a simple trip to the dairy for a carton of milk or a pack of cigarettes. It was absolutely one of the most bizarre scenes I had ever encountered, but, before I could process it all, my guide reappeared, looking a bit dishevelled.

'Shit, that was quick,' I remarked.

'I couldn't bloody get it to work, so she tossed me out,' he said without a hint of bashfulness. 'Fuck it, let's go to a bar. I know a place.'

It was a massive hall that reeked of beer and cigarette smoke, and was packed end to end with rather unsavoury-looking characters. But we did our best to blend in, and passed some time talking about home and work as we drank our way through beer after beer. At some point, we noticed two large German guys, standing on either side of us.

'Vere you from?' one asked.

'New Zealand,' I said.

'Ah … some big drinkers in Noi See-land,' he said, officially commencing an international drinking contest. I wanted no part of it, but my counterpart insisted.

'Silly German bastards,' he said. 'We'll show you how to drink.'

Beer has never really had much of an effect on me, and, even though we hadn't bothered to eat dinner before our arrival at the bar, these German guys were soon absolutely legless. I wasn't even really pissed, but our competitors were holding onto the bar for balance — down, but not quite out. My fellow Kiwi excused himself to go have a pee, and he seemed okay — but he never returned. I checked the loo, I checked outside: he had done a runner. I tried to ask the German guys where he might have gone, but at this point they were absolutely paralytic, unable to move, much less communicate in their native tongue or mine.

By this time it was about 2 am, and I was as sober as a judge, but I had no idea where my hotel was. The city was deathly quiet — no cabs, no tram, nothing. I figured I would just start walking in the hope that I would find someone or something that would give me a clue as to where I was headed. After about fifteen minutes of aimless wandering, an English-speaking cab driver picked me up and, after I told him the name of my hotel, was pleased to inform me that I had been walking in the wrong direction. I recounted the events of the evening for him, and he seemed to guffaw harder and harder at each point in the story. When he let me out at the hotel, he refused payment, saying he was pleased to have had such a good laugh.

The next morning, my Kiwi counterpart was supposed to pick me up after breakfast, but he never showed. In fact, I never saw him again. (The more I thought about it, the more I felt sure that he must have crawled out the window of the loo, because there was no way he could have made it past me in the bar. I actually did make telephone contact with him months later, back in New Zealand, but before I could find out from him what had happened, the first thing he said to me was: 'I don't want to talk about that night — at all.')

I was happy enough to put that experience in the past and catch up with Alex Giesen, who would spend the next ten days driving me from vineyard to vineyard and winery to winery. Along the way we even met Helmut Becker, still considered one of the foremost authorities on Riesling and Müller-Thurgau.

One of the things I will never forget was that Alex was wearing lederhosen — quite an unusual concept for a Kiwi. That aside, I have to think that Alex was preparing himself for life in New Zealand, because we drank nearly everything we came across — interrupted by brief episodes of inhaling steak and potatoes everywhere we went. I was getting a bit bored with it, as well as watching my waistline expand, so I asked if we could try something other than beef one night.

'Well, you know,' Alex said to me, 'in some restaurants we ate beef, in others we ate horse.'

'Really?' I asked.

'Yes, no one ever knows the difference!'

To this day I have no idea if he was just taking the piss, but somehow I don't think he was. Alex rather enjoyed my frequent miscommunications as we traversed the German countryside. One night, for instance, I accidentally ordered a giant carafe of ouzo in a Greek restaurant — Alex just smiled the entire time I tried to communicate with the waitress, knowing full well what a mess I had made of a simple interaction.

For every ounce of booze, beef and horsemeat absorbed, however, I took in an equal amount of knowledge. Everywhere we went, I saw the practices and techniques that we were aspiring to at home. It was like playing rugby with eight-year-olds one day and watching the All Blacks from the bench the very next. But perhaps most significant of all, I knew that my life among the vines would be all the more successful now that I had Alex as a friend and colleague. (It was only a matter of months after he dropped me off at a train station, to finish up my journey, that he and his brothers would make the move to New Zealand.)

As much as I found fun and education in Germany, I was eager to get home, be with my family again, get back to work, and employ as much of my new-found knowledge as Corbans could bear. I truly felt as if I were ready to help the company make a serious run at domination of the New Zealand wine industry.

Within twelve hours of my arrival home, Cathy gave birth to our daughter Sara. I barely had time to process our good fortune, however, as quite a bit had transpired at Corbans during my three-week absence — the most shocking development being Jim Hamilton's departure from the company. He had decided to quit and focus on developing his own vineyard. Jim had been running Corbans' vineyards nationally, operating out of Gisborne, so he was more tied into the political web in which Rothmans and Corbans were both tangled. Part of the problem was that Jim was the boss of Joe Corban, once upon a time the heir-apparent to Corbans. Jim knew about all the bad blood between the Corbans and their key stakeholders, where all the proverbial bodies were buried, and who was trying to gain leverage over each other and how — and he was tired of being caught in the middle of the daily power struggles.

I, of course, knew about none of this at first. Even when Joe Corban would come to Marlborough and have a look around, I remember being in awe and thinking, *Wow, that's Joe Corban ... in my vineyard!* But after Jim's departure I was summoned to Auckland, and the picture immediately started to become clear the instant I was offered the opportunity to replace Jim as Corbans' national vineyard manager.

I loved the job — far more than I thought I would, as I never imagined that corporate life would suit a guy who had got his start in the shearing sheds in the middle of nowhere. The one unfortunate part was that I had got quite friendly with the Corbans family, and one of the first orders I had to carry out was to sack Joe, since there wasn't really a role for him any longer. I got the sense that I was designated to be the triggerman since I was the new guy, so would not be as emotionally involved as everyone else. While that was probably true to some extent, over time I would learn that Corbans really needed to clean its house if it ever hoped to survive and thrive. It was the same old story as countless other industries had seen before: a wealthy entity (Rothmans) comes to the aid of another (Corbans), but the company that takes the bailout insists on carrying on as before, without changing its ways. Essentially, Rothmans had had enough, and concluded that the best way to ensure the security of the Corbans legacy and company was to relieve everyone with the family name of their duties.

That meant that all of a sudden I was looking after every Corbans vineyard and grower throughout the country. I was constantly bouncing around between Marlborough, Gisborne, Kumeu, Huapai, Henderson — all of them, other than Marlborough, buggered with phylloxera and growing varieties such as Gamay Noir, Seibel hybrids and Chasselas, which had virtually no use or customer appeal. The Henderson vineyards were practically in the middle of a housing development — so at least we were able to sell off that land and not have to worry about it any longer. But the rest needed to be either replanted or sold off (or both).

Running between all of these spots might sound a bit manic, but the great thing about being a part of a large company such as Rothmans was that I could always get where I needed to go by calling in the company plane. It was bloody fantastic: a Beechcraft King Air fitted out with big armchairs. It would take six passengers, although I am amazed that it ever even got into the air, considering how weighted down it was with all the liquor you could possibly want. And of course every spare slot was filled with packs of Rothmans cigarettes. If I needed to go to Gisborne, I would ring up and they would fly down and take me to Gisborne. Auckland? No problem, see you in ninety minutes. Plus, Rothmans owned the Park Royal and Travelodge hotels in Christchurch, Wellington and Hawke's Bay, so I never needed to fret about booking a hotel when I travelled for work.

I have no idea whether others in the company were afforded this sort of luxurious convenience, but I suspect not. Rothmans was a strange organisation and, looking back, I can't conceive of a sensible corporate structure in which a person at my position and level would be offered

The Rothmans plane, suitably registered RGA, at Woodbourne (Marlborough) Airport, 1986

such perks. But I suppose I fitted the mould, just being an extrovert, happy to pitch in and do anything, take responsibility, make decisions — it was the way I had been brought up, and there must have been something they appreciated about this. I was also included in many more boardroom gatherings — billowing with cigarette smoke, of course — than I ever should have been.

In or around these meetings I would occasionally encounter K.D. Butland, son of Sir Jack Butland, founder of Butland Industries, an Auckland packaged-food company that was tied to Rothmans (Sir Jack was a director of Rothmans, as was K.D., later). I have no idea what K.D. saw in me, but, for whatever reason, every so often I would get these strange calls at home: 'Mr Butland would like you to come up to Auckland to talk with him.' The plane would already be on its way to Marlborough, so I would drive over to the airport, hop on the Beechcraft, and be flown to his office in Auckland.

Butland was one of the richest people in New Zealand at that time, so I would be sitting in his office, talking around in circles with him about whatever he wanted to discuss, all the while quietly wringing my hands since it was like being in front of royalty.

'Mr Scott,' he would say with seeming randomness in one of these meetings, 'I'll get my chauffeur to take you to a friend of mine's property. Just have a look and tell me what you think, and what he could grow there.'

The first time he sent a chauffeur for me, I got in the front seat of the massive Vanden Plas. It's the sort of car that usually ferries around the villains in Bond films. The driver, Bill, gave me a strange look and said, 'I'm sorry, Mr Scott, but Mr Butland would prefer you sit in the back.'

'To be honest,' I said, 'I feel like a bit of a tosser back there. Can't we just say I'm the mechanic riding with you?'

'No, Mr Scott, you've got to sit in the back.'

I sighed and took my place, wondering whether the people we passed were muttering to themselves, 'I wonder who that wanker is?'

Everywhere I was taken, I was treated like royalty, since I was technically representing Mr Butland, as K.D. was always known. It never felt any less absurd each of the several times I was taken to look at people's places, meet them, have a cup of tea, walk around and then go back home. Nothing ever seemed to come of it that I knew of, although another half-dozen times or so Mr Butland sent me to look at businesses. And he never seemed to care what else I was busy with, which was usually more important.

One time I was out in the middle of the Rapaura vineyards, helping the crew install irrigation, since we were miles behind schedule and needed every available set of hands. Out of nowhere, the PA from our office drove up and said, 'Mr Butland really wants you in Auckland. The plane is on its way.' I was covered in dirt and incredibly stressed, since that part of the vineyard was really struggling without water. Yet I had less than an hour to run home, shower and change, then dash to the airport. The last place I ever expected I would be sent in such a hurry was to an agricultural breeding outfit. I had never seen so many people walking around in white coats. I was shown around the place in a Land Rover, out the back of the paddock, then over here, over there, while being told 'Here's what we plan to do out this way where all those sheds and concrete are now', and so on. I had to stay in Auckland overnight, and all I could think about was getting back to Rapaura to finish the immediate, important task at hand. But first I had to go and meet Mr Butland, who proceeded to ask all sorts of strange questions. All I could really say was, 'Well, it was very impressive ... lots of people in white coats, carrying clipboards.'

He nodded, scribbled some notes and sent me back home. I never heard another thing about it until two months later, when I read in the newspaper that the entire operation had been shut down. Obviously, the investors — Mr Butland perhaps being one of them, or maybe Rothmans — needed a reason to make their move, and might have used my uninformed assessment as part of their ammunition. Thankfully, it was the last time I would be sent on such a mission, and I was able to focus more on my real job from that point on.

One of Corbans' biggest problems, that I could see, became apparent right as we started getting grapes off Rapaura. We were selling them off, primarily the Sauvignon Blanc, and other wineries were getting the attention and gold medals for wines they had made from the grapes grown by my crews on land I had set up and was managing. To me, it was like a chef winning a prestigious culinary award when all he had done was sprinkle some parsley on the dish at the pass. So I and a few others in the Corbans hierarchy decided that we needed our own high-end label of vineyard-specific wines that could be sold in restaurants. There would be a Sauvignon Blanc, a Riesling and a Chardonnay from Marlborough, as well as a Cabernet Sauvignon from Gisborne. The only thing we had yet to figure out was what to name the new brand.

The first choice of a name was Settlement, but that one had already been registered in Australia. Around this same time I had been digging around the Rapaura property's old sheds and other structures, and I had found a

The entrance to the Stoneleigh vineyard in the late 1980s

stencil with the name 'Stoneleigh' on it. (The corner of the property, where the Matua winery sits today, is incredibly rocky, with hectare after hectare of round, smooth riverstones atop the surface of the dirt. The land, once irrigated, was perfectly suited to grapevines — especially Sauvignon Blanc.) I didn't particularly like the name at first, since I thought it sounded too English. However, it was decided that this would be the name of the wine, and it grew on me once I saw the label, which displayed the Stoneleigh name in the same fashion as the stencil. What I appreciated even more was that the Stoneleigh label was created to put the focus on the viticulturist, not the winemaker — so in a sense it was my name attached to the brand.

Rather amazingly, we were able to take the market by surprise with the Stoneleigh brand, as we managed to keep everything about it quiet until the day it launched in 1984; I even registered the brand to my home address so no one would find out what we were up to. And when Stoneleigh launched, it had an instant impact in the market, and was even recognised beyond the wine industry for the smart marketing and branding effort behind it.

To represent what we hoped to achieve with Stoneleigh, showing our best efforts from specific vineyard sites, it had been decided that the label should display the Richmond Range to the north of Marlborough, with the Gisborne trees in the foreground. With such an approach, Stoneleigh was the first New Zealand wine label that told the story, right on the front of the bottle, of where the wine came from — and thereby emphasised the importance of that knowledge in the customer's experience of the wine. It was a simple, subtle touch, but it was unlike anything the New Zealand wine industry had seen up to that point.

That label has remained much the same for three decades. Yet it pains me to think of how big Stoneleigh could have been. It's the embodiment of an incredible opportunity squandered, but then again, that's the story of the wine industry more often than not — there is always an ego, an idea or a series of unlucky events that tends to get in the way of progress or achievement. Stoneleigh should have been the flag-bearer for New Zealand wine. But, despite its longevity, it never got the chance to become a truly iconic brand. That honour would fall to Cloudy Bay, which rose on the back of Stoneleigh, with plenty of help from me — not all of it intentional, and virtually none of it foreseeable.

I DIGRESS ...

One of the best things about living and working in Marlborough is our quick and convenient access to the Sounds. Every warm-weather weekend, at least some or all members of our family spend as much time there as we can. It's a pity that most people's exposure to this beautiful area is a quick zig and zag through the waterways on the ferry between Wellington and Picton. With hundreds of coves, islands and inlets (not to mention the calm, clear water), the Sounds comprise one of the most beautiful and relaxing spots in all of New Zealand.

For many years, Cathy's family has owned a small bach off the Queen Charlotte Drive, not far from Picton. It is tucked along a steep, rocky private drive in a cluster of a half-dozen or so other houses separated by lush, thick vegetation. All of the houses are just steps away from the sand and water. Ours is tiny, with only one common room, a small kitchen and a tiny bedroom – altogether it's not much larger than a shipping container. For a long time, it was in a state of complete disrepair, although in recent years we have fixed it up and added a second, more modern one-bedroom bach behind it. Our kids and grandkids love spending summer weekends and

CLIMBING THE CORPORATE LADDER

holidays there, enjoying the sun and water. Cathy and her friends sometimes hole-up there for a couple of nights with some fashion magazines and a few bottles of bubbly. Occasionally Josh will head out from there on a small motorboat and fish for blue cod or dive for scallops.

Generally, I prefer spending time at the bach alone. It is one of the few places I can escape to and be left in peace to read, think or take an afternoon nap. The phone service is especially crap, so it is always certain that I won't be bothered by more than the sound of the wind, the call of a quail or the faraway hum of a boat's motor. Occasionally, though, we do host friends and wider family there, or maybe gather for an afternoon with the folks who own the other nearby houses. But that's not always so pleasant.

One time, we were invited to our neighbours' place on a sunny afternoon. For some reason they had brought with them their pet budgie, in a little wooden cage. We were sitting on the deck, enjoying some drinks, when out of nowhere a feral cat darted out from the bush. The poor budgie — alone and exposed, and several feet away from where we were all sitting around the table, drinking and gabbing — practically exploded in a cloud of feathers as the cat leaped at the cage. Everyone freaked out, and a sort of chaos ensued not unlike the scene with the killer bunny in *Monty Python and the Holy Grail*. The budgie was, amazingly, unharmed ... although quite likely psychologically damaged.

The cat scampered down the beach as our neighbour ran back inside to grab his .22 rifle, which he handed to me, assuming I'd be a good shot.

'Fucking feral cats,' someone mumbled. 'Eating all the native birds.'

'Bloody pests,' someone else muttered.

I have no idea why the rifle was handed to me. In a restaurant, handing me the wine list makes sense. I can only suppose that they thought I had a cooler head than anyone else, so the gun was in my hands. Despite my erratic aim, I took down the cat on the first shot, and received all sorts of congratulations and thank-yous from everyone for doing my part to conserve New Zealand's fragile, seriously threatened ecosystem. I handed the rifle back to its owner, then went to get a shovel to bury the cat. I dug a hole, pushed the bird-assaulter into the bottom, and covered it up. We all went back to our drinks, and did our best to console the owner of the budgie as well as move on to other topics of conversation.

The next morning we rose early for breakfast and a dip in the cold water. Even in summer, it has a refreshing chill that jolts you back to life, and gets you ready to enjoy the day. As we walked back up from the beach, we could see another neighbour's young daughter wandering between houses. This was typical for a summer weekend — there are always children out and about, playing in the sand or among the trees.

Her mouth was moving: she appeared to be saying something to us or someone else nearby, but we couldn't hear her over the sound of the wind and the waves. But as we got closer, all of the breath seemed to be sucked from our lungs at once as we heard her words: 'Here, kitty, kitty, kitty! Here, kitty, kitty, kitty!'

We stopped in our tracks, as much because of what she was saying, as where she was standing — right on top of the grave I had dug the day before.

'Hello,' she said to us with a beyond-her-years air of maturity and politeness. 'Have you seen my kitten?'

We were silent for what felt like an eternity.

'No, no,' we all seemed to be saying at once.

'But we'll come around if we see her,' I said.

'Thank you,' she said, as she wandered off. 'Here kitty, kitty, kitty!'

Allan Scott 2, cats O.

When our older daughter, Vic, got married, she and her husband, Dan, did what any newlywed couple does before having children of their own, which is to get a pet. They settled on a white, fluffy cat they named Paris — even though she was about as pleasant and cuddly as Invercargill.

Vic and Dan moved house quite a bit over the first couple of years, and eventually Paris wound up living with Cathy and me. I use the term 'living' somewhat loosely, because Paris always seemed to come and go of her own accord. She didn't live in the house, but the little diva would always show up when she wanted food or attention. Then she would bugger off again.

One day, she came back looking a bit ill. She was thin and more irritable than usual — almost like a Paris fashion model, now that I think of it.

'Look, you have to put Paris out of her misery,' Cathy said to me. It didn't help that Paris and our Jack Russell, Bella, were oil and water. To make matters worse, there is a small pond out the back of our house, and we had a feeling that Paris had been eating the ducklings. Cathy kept asking me to put Paris down, but every time I thought of it, she was nowhere to be found. (In truth, I had no desire to execute yet another house cat, so I never looked particularly hard.) And every time she did show up back at the house, sometimes with a small feather dangling from her chin, one look from me was all it took to send Paris dashing back out into the vineyard. She was as cunning as a cartload of monkeys.

A few weeks later, Cathy and I were heading off on holiday, so I rang Ra Hebberd, the vineyard manager at our family winery at the time (as well as a rugby mate of Josh's), and asked him to be on the lookout for Paris.

'We're going away,' I told him, 'so if you see Paris, can you just put a shot into her and make her disappear? I don't need to know the specifics, just make it so she doesn't show up again.'

'Sure, no problem,' Ra said.

A few days later he was working in the vines near our house when he caught a glimpse of Paris. He told Brian — our head vineyard manager and Cathy's brother-in-law — that he needed to go and take care of Paris for us, so he ran off to get his rifle. When he came back, Paris was sitting under the hedges near the house. He couldn't get too close since she would scamper off, so Ra kept his distance, drew a bead on her and fired the shot.

'You get her?' Brian asked when Ra went back to work.

'I definitely shot her, but I can't find her anywhere.'

Brian, not wanting us to come home to a dead cat on our doorstep, then gathered nearly the entire full-time vineyard crew to commence a search for Paris. Everyone was calling out for her and searching under the trees, in the hedges, among the vines — but a fluffy, white corpse was nowhere to be found. Eventually, everyone looked at each other, shrugged their shoulders and assumed that Paris had wandered off and would eventually die from her wound, lead poisoning or both. When Cathy and I returned home from holiday, Ra fronted up to tell me that he'd had a shot, was certain that he had hit Paris, but that she had done a runner. She might turn up dead eventually, maybe, but it was more likely that she had already been scooped up by a hawk. Whatever the case, I felt it best to spare Cathy the details.

'Has Ra taken care of Paris?' she asked me later.

'Yep. Yeah, yeah. Done,' I said.

'Are you sure?' she asked, perhaps because she knows me too well.

'Yes, it's fine,' I said. 'It's all done, all good.'

Two full months passed. Cathy and I were sitting in our living room, watching TV one night. The room has floor-to-ceiling windows on two sides, but after dark, with the lights on inside, each window is a black rectangle. Although you can't see anything outside, you can certainly hear ... especially when a set of claws is scratching at one of the windows.

'It's Paris!' Cathy screamed at me after she approached the glass and could get a glimpse outside. 'I thought Ra had done her!'

I turned on the outside light, and there was Paris. Cathy went off, screaming at me to put the pathetic, meowing mess — dragging one of her hind legs as if it were an anchor — out of its misery. I think Paris understood every word of Cathy's tirade, because the now far-less-glamorous-looking moggy scampered off as soon as I went to get my .22-calibre rifle.

So there I was, stalking around the outside of our house in the evening, trying to catch up with this elusive, shaggy, dirty, miserable ball of fluff. As if I were in an old gangster film, I made it professional once I had caught up with her — one shot, right to the head. It felt every bit as unpleasant as you would expect, so I turned around and walked back inside, somewhat relieved that it was all over.

'Have you shot her?'

'Yes, I have,' I said as I put away the gun.

'Well, have you buried her?'

'Just let me finish watching this thing on TV,' I said. 'She's not going anywhere.'

'But you did shoot her?'

'Yes, I saw her bloody dead,' I said, getting annoyed. 'I stood right over her.' I might even have turned up the volume on the TV.

A few minutes later, Cathy went outside to pull the washing off the clothesline. That's when I heard a horrific shriek.

'You haven't bloody killed her!' Cathy screamed, tears streaming down her cheeks as she ran back inside. 'What the fuck?!'

'But I saw her stretched out on the ground!' I said. 'I killed her.'

'You haven't!'

I grabbed the gun again and went back outside to see Paris, looking especially angry with me, as only a feline who has been shot and left for dead – twice – can. At the sight of me, she hissed, then took off into the woodshed behind the garage. This time I shot her at point-blank range, dragged out her corpse, dug a hole, buried her and stomped on it. I was half tempted to fire a few more bullets into the ground, just to be certain.

'Have you shot her this time?' Cathy asked me sarcastically, as I came back inside.

The worst part, of course, is that I have never told Vic any of this about her old cat. I have been meaning to find a way to tell her for years now, but I guess this will have to do.

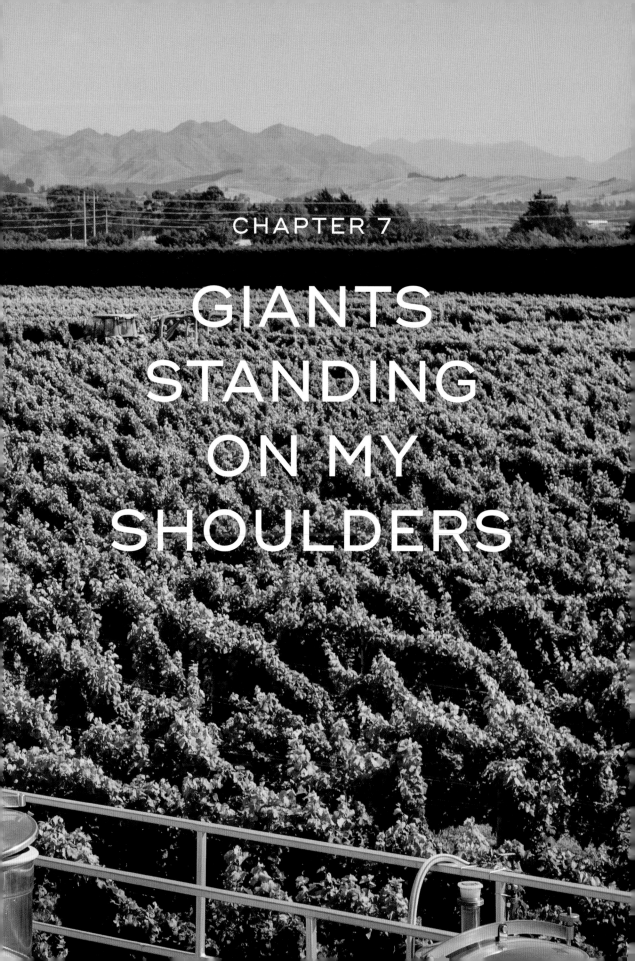

CHAPTER 7

GIANTS STANDING ON MY SHOULDERS

NEARLY EVERY ARTICLE OR BOOK WRITTEN ABOUT
New Zealand wine mentions — and overly romanticises — one particular anecdote. It is a tale in which four Kiwi winemakers with a bottle of 1983 Marlborough Sauvignon Blanc in the boot of their car happen upon Australian winemaker David Hohnen, founder of the Cape Mentelle winery at Margaret River. They give the wine to Hohnen, and he loves what he tastes so much that he then leads his people across the Australian deserts, waves his arms in the air to part the Tasman Sea, and then leads the Chosen Ones to Marlborough to create the holy state of Cloudy Bay.

Okay, I jest. But while it is true that David was inspired to expand to Marlborough after he had tasted this particular wine, no one ever seems to bother telling the rest of the story. It is not a particularly riveting tale full of intrigue, pathos and drama, complete with a cast of loose-moraled Bond girls ... mostly because I'm involved. While there is no question that the Cloudy Bay winery would have been a success with or without me (especially given that in Kevin Judd, James Healy and Ivan Sutherland the

171

winery boasted the most talented winemaking team in New Zealand), it wouldn't be where it is geographically, right at the heart of Marlborough, if not for the deals I orchestrated between David Hohnen and Corbans. David had the intelligence and experience to send Cloudy Bay into the stratosphere, but he was also sharp enough to know that his cause would be advanced all the more quickly if he had the help of someone like me to build the launch pad in just the right place.

After the visit from the four Kiwis, David came to Auckland in 1984 to attend the annual wine show. At first, he figured he would try to find some grapes to buy and make some Marlborough Sauvignon Blanc under contract; it was just a matter of finding the right grapes and a place to ferment the juice. He poked around the show, tasted this wine, shook that hand and eventually met winemaker Kevin Judd, who was working for Selaks in Auckland. David had also scheduled an appointment to meet with Corbans' winemaker, the German fellow Norbert Seibel, who had arranged my excursion to Switzerland and Germany.

I happened to be in Auckland at the time as well, and Norbert told me that an Australian winemaker had asked to see him. Norbert surmised that David wanted to buy some grapes, which meant he probably should meet with me instead. Part of my job involved relationship management with Corbans' growers, as well as arranging the sale of grapes to small players such as Ernie Hunter of Hunter's Wines, and larger ones such as Selaks and Nobilo.

In truth, I had never heard of David Hohnen at this point, although I probably should have. His Cape Mentelle Cabernet had won a prestigious trophy in an Australian wine competition two years in a row, a feat as rare then as it is now. After such a run of success, it made sense that he would have grander ambitions than simply to make a Marlborough Sauvignon Blanc as a side venture. Nevertheless, that was his relatively modest initial proposal, and he wanted to know the odds of Corbans selling him the grapes he would need.

At the Tourist Hotel Corporation New Zealand Wine Awards, mid-1980s

'Pretty good chances,' I told him, because at this point Corbans needed to keep its coffers full to support the burgeoning Stoneleigh brand. Nothing sucks cash from a winery like launching a new brand, and one of the best ways to support it is to make less wine than you project you can sell, then let the market dictate what your demand will ultimately be. Meanwhile, you keep the cashflow strong by selling off excess grapes because, after all, it's far better to have not enough wine than to have too much. Around this time, Corbans was bordering on being desperate to sell fruit.

What I didn't anticipate, however, was that the Corbans hierarchy would be sceptical — even borderline paranoid — about selling grapes to this Australian who had seemed to materialise out of nowhere. But it turned out their first instinct was the right one.

However, while most other people probably would have told David 'Sorry' and sent him on his way to find another grape supplier, I had a sixth sense about him. David is a charmer, down-to-earth and friendly, but I did get the feeling that he wasn't going to be easily deterred — and that he was a sharp operator who wouldn't have made the trip all the way from Margaret

River if he wasn't serious about finding success in New Zealand. There had to be more to him than just wanting a load of Sauvignon Blanc on which he could slap his own label. So when I delivered to David the unfortunate news that Corbans wasn't interested in selling him grapes, I suggested he come down to Marlborough for a visit and stay at our house. He took me up on the invitation, and arrived with Kevin Judd in tow.

David was immediately won over by the Marlborough scene, perhaps because what he saw was a version of Margaret River in a period of infancy that he had missed, having been born too late. Marlborough presented a chance to get in on the ground floor — David saw the region's potential in a way that few others could have at the time, because he knew what it was like to be in a wine region during its ascent. He knew instantly that all of the elements required for Marlborough to succeed were already in place — he just needed to find some land to buy if he was going to be a part of it, never mind be its flag-bearer.

During his stay at our house, David admitted that he had not only hired Kevin Judd to be his founding winemaker, but that his plans were far more ambitious than he had initially let on. He also asked whether I would be interested in managing the grape-growing side of things for his new venture.

My answer, without hesitation: 'Shit, yeah.'

There was a particular property I knew of near the Fairhall vineyard that would be ideal, I told David, and I was relatively certain that I could get it, since Cathy and I had had a sort of handshake option to buy it at one point. However, it turned out that the lawyer representing the owner of the land had the first option and had subsequently bought the property for himself. I sent David to see the lawyer, but he turned him down flat, leaving him back at square one.

I knew that Corbans was looking to divest itself of some land holdings, but I knew I had to be careful, as I had a genuine conflict of interest. I suggested, though, that David might be able to devise an approach in a way that would meet Corbans' most pressing needs. For example, Corbans was desperate to part with a tank of dry Sémillon sitting in the winery that Norbert had made. I actually loved that wine, and I couldn't figure out why no one inside or out of Corbans wanted it. I arranged to get a sample of the wine to David Hohnen, who agreed with my assessment of it. That wine became, in fact, the very first Cloudy Bay release — a Marlborough County Sémillon. (It was delicious, even if Corbans was ultimately correct in terms of its market appeal, because it didn't wind up selling all that well.)

Corbans was also eager to press on with the construction of the Stoneleigh winery, as originally intended, at the corner of Jacksons and Rapaura roads.

The Corbans vineyard crew enjoying a break on a hot day

Corbans didn't necessarily need to sell land to fund the winery's construction, but it certainly couldn't hurt. In the meantime, it wanted to find a way to make Stoneleigh Sauvignon Blanc in Marlborough instead of sending all of the grapes up to Gisborne or Auckland. I suggested to David that Corbans might be more willing to sell him the Sauvignon Blanc grapes he needed to start Cloudy Bay if he bought some land as well. The particular block I suspected Corbans might be willing to part with was the one where the Cloudy Bay winery sits today, on Jacksons Road, right in the heart of Marlborough.

'Okay,' David said to me. 'I'll think about that.'

'One caveat, though,' I told him. 'There's a 20-acre [8-hectare] appendage to the property I developed that was originally intended to handle the wastewater from where the Stoneleigh winery was to be built. If the deal with Corbans goes through and you get the property, you sell those 20 acres [8 hectares] to me.'

I wish, as I am sure David does, that it had all been that simple. And it nearly was, with Corbans agreeing to sell to Cloudy Bay the land as well as the grapes it needed to launch its Sauvignon Blanc ahead of the winery's construction; in return, Stoneleigh's Sauvignon Blanc would be made at Cloudy Bay's new winery. The one surprise was that David's brother Mark, who handled their company's finances, initially refused to sell the 20-acre (8-hectare) road-front appendage to Cathy and me.

'You'll have to take one of the blocks in behind,' David said, knowing full well that the land was where Cathy and I intended to build a new house for our family.

Bloody Australians, can't ever trust them, was pretty much all I was thinking, even though I said just about everything but that. I believe David genuinely felt bad about the situation, but he insisted that there wasn't much he could do, even though I had made it possible for him to acquire the land he needed to get Cloudy Bay off the ground. Plus, I was still on the hook to develop and plant his vineyard, as well as my now-undetermined section, all while still working for Corbans.

'Who wants to live in a vineyard, next to a winery, anyway?' David asked me.

It was not a particularly fashionable notion at the time, as grape-growing and winemaking were no more romantic or less industrial in perception than milking cows or shearing sheep. I believed that would change over time, however, so I held my ground. Eventually David and his brother relented — I suspect, in part, because Kevin Judd rang David and let him have it. Although Kevin grew up in Australia (he's English by birth), he had lived in New Zealand for long enough to know that, while Kiwis and Aussies both conduct business on handshake deals, those deals actually mean something in New Zealand. David and Mark backed down, but on one condition: Cathy and I would have to pay about 25 per cent above the market rate for the land, which around that time was $4,000 per acre ($1,600 per hectare). It completely clobbered us, but we knew we had to

Our 'Bubble Busters' wine-tasting team at the National Wine Options in Wellington: left to right, Daniel Le Brun, me, Adele Le Brun and Cathy

take the deal or lose out on the land forever. To finance the purchase and have some money left over for the construction of a new home, we put a relatively outrageous price on our Old Renwick Road house as it went on the market. We were extremely lucky, as a buyer arrived, seemingly out of nowhere, and paid the asking price in cash. He fell in love with the place on sight, and he still lives there today.

Then we got even luckier. Towards the end of 1983 and into 1984, interest rates in New Zealand went sky-high overnight, due to a very fragile economy and massive deflation. When investors become concerned that a government cannot pay its debts, the bond rates skyrocket, with consumer-banking interest rates typically following suit. This was a bad thing for small businesses, particularly wineries such as Hunter's Wines, which was struggling to pay its loans as interest rates climbed above 20 per cent. But for Cathy and me, who had no business or debt of our own, it was an

An aerial view of our winery site on Jacksons Road

outstanding opportunity. We had put our money in the bank at night, and pulled it out the next morning at a gain that otherwise would have taken months or even years to accrue. Despite incurring a rather hefty tax bill, over six months we nearly doubled our nest egg.

This allowed us to begin construction on our new home at the same time as ground was broken for the Cloudy Bay winery, in 1985. That should have been comfortable, what with everything sorted between us and David Hohnen, but the Corbans brass were none too pleased that I had essentially been wearing two hats while I was on their watch — even though, in the end, the company had got what it wanted in terms of a land sale and a new home for the Stoneleigh winemaking. I was on shaky ground with my employer, but, I have to admit, I somewhat relished the excitement of wheeling and dealing, which I probably did more of than grape-growing from one year to the next at Corbans.

I loved the idea of charting my own path, and Cathy and me building something for our family and our future, even though I still genuinely loved the corporate life I was afforded at Corbans — in no small part because I found it was possible to do my day job as well as have my finger in plenty of other pies. I knew everything that was happening in Marlborough wine that was good, bad or ugly, and I usually managed to find a way to be involved — for Corbans' benefit, my own, or both. As opportunities presented themselves over the next few years, I leaped at every one.

The biggest of them all came in 1986.

What I couldn't have predicted — no one could have, I believe — is that the 1986 vine-pull would be the jolt we all needed, both on an individual level, for anyone willing and smart enough to see and take advantage of what was happening, as well as for the Marlborough wine industry as a whole. If you are not familiar with it, the vine-pull scheme came about when the government concluded in 1985 that New Zealand was experiencing a wine glut. The solution would be, starting in early 1986, to pay wineries and growers a per-hectare subsidy of $6,175 to pull out their grapevines.

Now, every wine region has its one moment in history that is the result of complete and utter stupidity, only for everyone to turn a corner and see how the local industry has vastly improved soon after. For America, it was Prohibition. For Europe, it was the spread of phylloxera and all the silly methods and experiments attempted to save the wine industry before an American viticulturist invented grafting. For New Zealand, it was the vine-pull — a purely political and poorly conceived and executed scheme that ultimately had a positive effect, contrary to the plan's original intent. Just as with most political decisions, there was a symptom, a cause and a prescribed solution — and none of them had anything to do with the other in leading to a decision that would give growers a windfall for ripping their vines from the earth.

First, to argue that there was a glut is ridiculous. While it is true that many New Zealand wineries were struggling and that cask-wine consumption was quickly becoming less fashionable, many wineries were doing just fine. Corbans continued to experience a number of difficulties, while Seagram had decided that it had had enough and had divested itself of Montana. But there were plenty of bright spots. Ernie Hunter, for example, took home three trophies — including the best wine of the show — at the London Wine Fair in 1985 for his Fumé Blanc, so it wasn't as if the world was unaware of the progress we were making as an industry. David Hohnen showed up and got Cloudy Bay going, so clearly he saw some promise, too. Daniel Le Brun, meanwhile, was already showing that he could make sparkling wine in Marlborough as good as any from his home region of Champagne.

Most growers and winemakers had already figured out by 1985 that Sauvignon Blanc was going to be the star of the Marlborough show — not Cabernet, Chenin Blanc or Müller-Thurgau. By this time, almost everyone in Marlborough had at least a decade's worth of experience in growing and vinifying multiple different varieties. We knew what worked well and what didn't, what sold and what didn't. Riesling showed lots of promise, but Sauvignon Blanc not only performed exceptionally well in Marlborough, it could also be cropped at a very high yield and still deliver excellent quality. Any experienced or sensible grower knew this well before 1985, but some simply wanted to keep their heads tucked in the sand rather than commit to the time and expense of replanting. Others just weren't particularly good at making wine, selling it, or both. But none of this meant that there was an industry-wide glut.

However, a few high-profile and politically connected wineries were experiencing trouble — notably Villa Maria, which had gone into receivership. Much like when General Motors faced collapse in America in 2008, Villa

Our property planted with cherry trees, and the Cloudy Bay winery beyond

Maria couldn't go down here in New Zealand in 1985 without a dedicated effort being made to save it, as it wasn't the sort of company that could disappear overnight without anyone noticing. One of the industry's biggest players being on the brink of going belly-up is enough to sell a nervous, agriculture-driven government on the notion that there is a problem requiring intervention, glut or no glut. (This was more than a bit ironic, given that the new Labour Government at the time professed itself to be laissez-faire, and generally pursued a departure from agricultural subsidies and farm-friendly policies.)

So it came as no surprise that the scheme was implemented hastily and with little consultation with industry and economic experts before it was announced. The vine-pull scheme, it had been determined, was the best and fastest way to save the industry as well as reduce New Zealand's vineyard land by 25 per cent.

As we all know, it accomplished nothing of the sort. (The exceptions were Hawke's Bay and Gisborne, where there was some initial reduction of vineyard land, but much of that land was already buggered with phylloxera anyway.) The main reason why Marlborough remained the same size in planted vineyard hectares is that the scheme contained no requirements in terms of what was to be done with the land once the vines were pulled. This meant, of course, that any enterprising, smart grower or winery could rip out Müller-Thurgau vines one day, collect a cheque from the government the next, and replant the entire property with Sauvignon Blanc the day after that, perhaps even at an immediate profit. Some people even bought planted, productive vineyards, then took the subsidy to rip out the vines and immediately came out ahead on the investment — often using some or all of the subsidy to replant right away. Everywhere you looked, Peter was being robbed to pay Paul.

In the decades since, many have stated that it was widely known that New Zealand was mostly producing mediocre-quality, uninteresting wines, and that the vine-pull was intended by the government to facilitate the shift away from Müller-Thurgau and towards Sauvignon Blanc. I seriously doubt that anyone in government actually believed that vineyards would simply be ripped out and replanted. If that is what they thought would happen, everyone should have been paid to replant with Sauvignon Blanc in a purely straightforward manner. Essentially, that is what happened anyway — but anyone who tells you that the vine-pull was conceived or executed intelligently by the government, much less that the intentions of the scheme were sincere, is delusional at best.

Corbans was at an interesting crossroads through all this. The company was having trouble selling wine, like several others, but most of its problems were with Rothmans, which was getting a bit testy since it wasn't seeing a quick return on its investment. (I don't think this ever has been proven possible in the wine industry, anywhere in the world.) Corbans survived the mid-1980s turmoil largely by selling off land — most notably the Moorland

The newly constructed Cloudy Bay winery in 1985

block where the Allan Scott winery sits today. Cathy and I went into partnership with Kevin Peterson, the former general manager of Corbans, to buy all 24 hectares. Over the next four years we would go through multiple subdivisions, replantings and sales of several sections of the property to various parties. To tell the truth, I'm not sure how we kept track of things, considering how many times and in how many places we carved off chunks for other buyers; sometimes we even bought back blocks, subdivided or replanted, then sold them again. All the while, though, we kept the road-front block where our winery sits today. That entire area was already planted with Riesling when we bought it, and we sold off the grapes each year to the Seifried Estate Winery in Nelson. This allowed us to keep our payments flowing to the bank — and keep our shirts.

If that — plus my involvement with Cloudy Bay — didn't make my employer nervous, my next move most certainly did: essentially, I became the first shareholder in the Grove Mill winery.

As Corbans was selling off land, its growers were getting more and more nervous. A big winery decreasing its vineyard holdings sends only one message to the contract growers: we need fewer grapes. So I wasn't at all surprised when one of the growers informed me that some of them were banding together to launch a winery of their own. He wanted to know whether I was interested in being a partner.

'Sure, I'd be more than interested,' I said.

At this point, you might be wondering if I ever decline a proposition. Admittedly, it's rare — and Cathy will be the first to say that it's probably my worst trait, the one that always gets us into the greatest amount of trouble. In fact, we had got involved in so many deals by then that we realised that, along with the building of our house, they would make it difficult for us to pay Vic's boarding-school fees — and she was just about to head off to Christchurch.

I pressed forward nonetheless, and helped the growers find a spot that would be suitable for a winery. It was quite an eclectic, smart group of stakeholders, including a very entrepreneurial local lawyer named Don Holden, as well as Rex Brooke-Taylor, who eventually went on to build the Framingham winery. There were several other well-known local families involved; some Cathy and I were comfortable working with, others not so much. Don drafted all of the agreements, which all of us signed, but nothing really moved forward due to a lack of cash. The first lease on the building that was intended to house the Grove Mill winery was $3,000 per month, which I paid out of my own pocket.

Cathy was cross with me, to say the least, since we had plenty of bills of our own to pay. I still felt as if the project had a future, but I realised that we couldn't keep paying into it forever with no plan as to when we would see a return. I couldn't progress as a smaller version of Rothmans, just sinking money into Corbans, with no immediately foreseeable end-game. I pulled out as a few more shareholders came in to keep the project afloat, but, before I left, the group asked whether I knew anyone who might be interested in being the winemaker. One name immediately came to mind.

The first load of grapes is delivered to the Cloudy Bay winery.

I recommended Dave Pearce, who was making wine for Corbans in the North Island. In all honesty, I didn't think he would be interested in such a big leap of faith — but he didn't hesitate in the slightest. Dave became the founding winemaker, and would remain at Grove Mill for more than twenty-five years, making him the longest-serving winemaker that I am aware of in Marlborough. Dave was making what I consider to be some of the best Marlborough wines throughout the 1980s and 1990s, and he also mentored an entire generation of winemakers, many of whom still work in the region today.

His run of success, in fact, is emblematic of something very important in the history of Marlborough wine: while Montana put the first stake in the ground, Corbans is where all of the region's true talents cut their teeth. As well as Dave Pearce, they included James Healy, who joined Kevin Judd at Cloudy Bay early on (and later went on to found Dog Point Vineyard); Bob Campbell, New Zealand's second Master of Wine and our foremost wine critic, who got his start at Montana but made a name for himself at

Corbans; Simon Waghorn, winemaker for Whitehaven as well as his own brand, Astrolabe; and Glenn Thomas, a Roseworthy classmate of Kevin Judd's, who joined us at Corbans in Gisborne as the first winemaker for Stoneleigh, before he moved to Vavasour in the late 1980s and pioneered wine-growing in the Awatere Valley. At one point or another, and especially during the second half of my tenure at Corbans, I worked with many of them as their careers and profiles grew.

All of us, however, had one particular thing in common: we all knew when and how to take our exit cues. Mine was probably more obvious than anyone else's.

Corbans' management were none too pleased when they found out that I was connected with the mass exodus of the company's growers to Grove Mill. It wasn't the straw that broke the camel's back, but my bosses wanted a genuine, straight answer from me: are you leaving or staying?

At first, I said I wanted to stay. But, in truth, Corbans was making the alternative decision easier with each passing day. The business side of the winery was becoming thoroughly unpleasant. Cooks, a smaller company with a winery in Hawke's Bay, was looking for a general manager of sorts. I admired their work, in part because their wine quality was higher than ours at Corbans, so the job held appeal at least in that respect. I applied, but was told that I was overqualified for the role — which is probably just as well, since Corbans eventually acquired Cooks. (I would have wound up right back in the fold or, worse, made redundant.) Shortly after that happened, I experienced a sense of the new world order — and I didn't like what I saw one bit.

At this time, Cooks was being directed by a hard-nosed businessman named George Exton. I was invited to attend the first meeting between

Corbans and the Cooks' growers committee, with Exton handling the introductions. After initial pleasantries were exchanged, he let the verbal assault begin, telling all of the growers what a bunch of bastards they were to deal with. He was incredibly abrasive if not downright abusive, and seemed hellbent on driving his growers into the ground — emotionally as well as financially. As the growers marched out of the meeting, the last one slammed the door hard behind him. I felt that Exton had had no reason to behave as he did; after the antagonised and upset growers had left, he just said to me calmly, 'They're all assholes, and you have to treat them like it.' It was as if he was trying to train dogs to not pee on a rug.

With my siblings John, Rosemary, and Ken at our mother Isa's seventy-fifth birthday

To repair the damage, I visited the growers one by one, all the way through to Christmas Eve, to get them back on our side. I went around to each grower's house and eventually was able to put their minds at ease and get them back on board. I started with the one who had slammed the door. He told me that I needed to build a personal, trusting relationship with each grower — that it never works when you get them all in a room, as it encourages a mob mentality.

I was quite pleased to have settled things down, but when I got back to work I never heard a 'Thanks' or a 'Good job'. That's really when I started to think that I'd had enough of life at Corbans. I was still a bit conflicted and frightened of the unknown, but my hesitations evaporated entirely in 1987.

Ernie Hunter, founder of Hunter's Wines, was one of my best mates. He was a magnanimous fellow who attracted new friends everywhere he went, locally or globally. He was known to enjoy a drink, too, but his presence lit up every room in which he ever set foot. Whether he was coming around for dinner or meeting up at the pub, I always knew I was in for a great time, full of laughter. His energy could be overwhelming, but anyone who met Ernie even once could never possibly forget him.

'Allan,' he said one day over the phone. 'I gaht a wee prah-blem.' (After decades in New Zealand, his Irish accent was still thicker than mashed spuds.)

Each vintage, Ernie had bought grapes from Corbans. He had a wish-list of the varieties he wanted, and I had told him that he could buy some of Corbans' crop of Gewürztraminer. Corbans, however, then decided that he couldn't have a single grape of any variety, despite my promise. I had been overruled.

All of the large wineries at the time were beginning to see what was happening throughout Marlborough, which was simply that smaller players, such as Ernie, were making better wines. While in most industries there is a belief that a rising tide lifts all boats, the bigger wineries were having none of it. I attended a meeting at Corbans where I made as solid a case for Ernie as I could, but the top brass wouldn't buy it: they were determined to keep control of the supply of grape varieties that were popular and scarce, rather than look inwards and get their own houses in order. I was bound by company rules, so there was nothing I could do for Ernie.

'This is *bullshit!*' he screamed at me when he arrived at my house, his face beet-red.

'I'm sorry, Ernie. Truly,' I said to him. 'There's nothing I can do. I can't get you the grapes.'

'We shook on it!' he screamed, the typically charming Ernie nowhere to be found.

'I know we did, but they won't let me give you the grapes.'

'Fuck them!' he screamed. '*You're* in charge, *you* make the decisions. Not them!'

'It's completely out of my control' was all I could muster.

'No,' he said, starting to calm down. 'You're a weak-willed *bastard*. You just don't do that to your mates.'

'I just came from my bosses, Ernie. They won't let me do it.'

Ernie never took 'no' for an answer, and that's what everyone loved about him. It's why he sold so much wine around the world, everywhere he went, and why buyers always came back for more. This time, though, he knew that nothing he could say or do would result in the grapes he needed arriving at his winery. As he stormed off, he said he would never speak to me again — and he was right about that. He was dead a month later, the result of a car accident on the road from Christchurch back up to Marlborough. (His wife, Jane, battling against the odds and everyone's assumptions, continued the winery, and with great success. She has since received a Queen's Honour for her services to the viticulture industry, and in 2013 became the first woman inducted into the New Zealand Wine Hall of Fame.)

To this day I go over that situation with Ernie in my mind every time I deal with a difficult problem, even all these years later. I think there is always a diplomatic solution, and I can't help but wonder that I perhaps had the skills at the time to make both sides happy but lacked the confidence to try harder than I did. Sometimes, though, no matter what position you hold in a large, corporate hierarchy, confidence and belief in your skills can be the first thing to suffer.

That was all the more true when, around this same time, I was moved under Kerry Hitchcock, who has had a long career in New Zealand winemaking and management — first at Cooks, then Corbans after the acquisition. (He was also one of the four Kiwis who introduced David Hohnen to New Zealand wine.) I like Kerry, a good-time Charlie, and he and I are still friendly today. But I regarded him more as an equal than as a boss. I usually preferred

Collecting wine awards with Corbans' general manager, Paul Treacher (centre), and the company's chief winemaker, Kerry Hitchcock

working for a mentor figure, such as Jim Hamilton or Cathy's father or even Jack Denham, my first boss on the farm in Canterbury — someone who really knew everything happening from grape to bottle. I also felt that, even though I was getting my hands dirty literally and figuratively, including organising all of our growers (no one else had taken any interest), my skills and experience for a top job in Corbans were being unfairly overlooked. It didn't matter anyway, as less than two months later everything was reorganised and I was shuffled out from under Kerry to report directly to the general manager, Paul Treacher. However, rather than being recognised or rewarded for the work I was doing, it felt as if I was simply one of many chess pieces being moved around, and that no player had a simple, straightforward, defined objective.

In early 1988, the ground was finally broken on the Stoneleigh winery, with Kerry and Alan McCorkindale in charge of construction. I didn't know a whole lot about winery configuration, but even the untrained eye could see from the plans that the building would be appalling — as ugly as it was

The Stoneleigh winery, soon after it was completed in 1989

nonsensical. I was asked where in the facility I wanted my office to be, but all I could think was *I don't want a bloody office.* Yet I was soon to be forced into one anyway.

While construction was underway, a Rothmans executive came down to check in on things. He had seen our newly built house from the road, and said to me with no embarrassment or hesitation whatsoever: 'How can you afford that house on your salary?'

'I work hard, I hope to think,' I said, somewhat shocked at the inappropriateness of the question.

'You have to be doing something illegal — into drugs or stealing.'

'Why would you say that?' I asked, completely taken aback.

'Nobody can do what you've done with what you say your background is. Nobody works hard to do whatever you did.'

I didn't feel the need to justify myself to anyone, much less this guy who didn't know me well or work directly with me. I didn't tell him that Cathy

Our house in Jacksons Road under construction in 1985

and I had juggled multiple jobs for most of our lives, or that we had taken advantage of interest rates as any smart person would have in the mid-1980s. I didn't tell him that I had worked hard at building relationships and contributing to the success of others with the belief that what goes around, comes around. I simply told the executive a part of the truth, which was that we had a nice house because we had made a decent amount selling the one we had had before. He shrugged his shoulders, as if my explanation made no sense and that I had confirmed all of his suspicions about me.

Fucking asshole, I thought to myself as he walked off.

Cathy's father always used to say to me: 'Never stay still. Always use one stepping stone to get to the next stepping stone. Take the slight risk with it, but so long as it's a calculated risk, you'll be fine.' In 1988, I told Cathy that I wanted nothing to do with Corbans any longer. We were making about the same amount as my salary on the grapes we were selling from our own property across the street from the house, as well as the vines surrounding our house, so we could survive a short-term hit to our income.

I rang the Corbans office in Auckland and told them I had had enough. You may recall that Montana had given me a silver platter and a pair of beautiful claret jugs upon my departure from the company, even though all I had really done was herd cats for several years — we had grown hardly any grapes that could be made into wine. Yet at Corbans I had built the Marlborough vineyards from the ground up, I had conducted research, I had worked with the growers and kept them happy, I had helped the company sell off land, and I even went on ridiculous errands for the corporate overlords, whenever or wherever they asked. For my dedication, Corbans gave me a framed photo of somewhere in the Marlborough Sounds. I put it in the rubbish bin a few days later.

I DIGRESS ...

There has long been a joke in California and Oregon that grapes are the 'other' crop. Just keep that in mind for a moment.

Around the time we were working on planting the vineyards surrounding our newly constructed house and the Cloudy Bay winery next door, we left a small paddock in between our two properties, about 100 metres from our house. It was planted neck-high in wheat, somewhat densely planted. It was a complete afterthought, a bit of land I would walk by or cruise past on the tractor and be reminded, Oh right, I need to do something with that. It turned out, however, that it served quite a good purpose that I hadn't thought of until one day, when the telephone rang.

I answered to hear a somewhat unsettled fellow on the other end of the line — a farmer who lived up the road. He and I knew each other by name and sight, but that's about all. He explained that he was raising some turkeys to fatten up for Christmas, but they had escaped from his paddock and run onto our land.

'I'd got them cornered, I thought, and then they ran into that patch of wheat you have back behind your house,' he said.

'Okay, well, no problem,' I replied, wondering what this was all about.

'Yes, well, it's just that ... I'm really sorry ... I wasn't interfering, I wasn't spying — I swear. And I won't tell anyone, I promise.'

I paused for a moment, which only seemed to make him more nervous.

'It's okay,' I said. 'But I don't really understand what you're talking about.'

'I found them,' he said, a tremble in his voice.

'The turkeys?' I asked. 'Well, that's good ...'

'No, no,' he said. 'I found your marijuana plants. I swear I won't tell anyone. I'm so sorry, really. But I just thought I'd let you know, in case you came around and saw the footprints.'

I immediately burst out laughing. 'Well,' I said, once I was able to catch my breath, 'they aren't my plants. But I appreciate you letting me know that someone's growing them behind my house.'

The farmer's relief was palpable, even along the telephone line. He was so paranoid when he had first rung, though, that I wouldn't have been surprised if he partook occasionally himself. I never did find out who the plants belonged to, and even though I had my suspicions I didn't look into it very hard.

I have never been a drug guy — I wouldn't know which end of the joint to smoke, as they say — and I don't have strong feelings about those who do enjoy it or get some medicinal benefit from cannabis. But marijuana is a major problem in wine regions, particularly in Californian vineyards, because marijuana not only thrives in a similar kind of climate, but it is a very thirsty plant. Pot-growers like to find the far corners of vineyards and tap into the vineyards' irrigation lines. Many vineyards are so deep into rough, remote country that no one notices the marijuana fields for weeks, months or even years. But the owner of the land winds up with a hefty water bill.

Here in Marlborough, we seldom find marijuana plants nowadays. Sometimes we used to find them down by a creek that runs near the bottom of our vineyard, in the riverbed — likely planted by boys working on the Air Force base adjacent to the airport. Even so, the plants were scraggly-looking and probably never productive, much less potent.

Funnily enough, about ten years later, that farmer came to work for us on a casual basis, then became permanent. He's now one of the most reliable and trusted members of our staff — and I know I never need worry about something other than grapes growing behind the house.

CHAPTER 8

LIVING AMONG LEGENDS

I HAVE KEPT A DAILY DIARY SINCE ABOUT THE LATE
1970s. Many of the pages for each day of the year are blank, while others
are, one could argue, a robust history of the Marlborough region. Take, for
example, this entry from 1992: *Bottled Riesling at Highfield, not a good day.* Or
this one from August 1998: *Everybody came to our house for drinky-poos.*

Believe it or not, though, for every silly, context-lacking entry such as these
two, there are a dozen more that, when I scribbled them at the time, felt
like simple, straightforward recountings of the business of the day — lunch
with this winemaker or a meeting with that grower. Looking at the diaries
today, however, they comprise quite a clear record of who was doing what
in New Zealand wine, when, where and why.

After I left Corbans in 1988, I teamed up with Pete Masters, my foreman
from Corbans, to form Mascott Partners as a grapevine nursery. I had the
ideal land at our newly purchased Jacksons Road property, and we had the
available stock to make rooted cuttings, as phylloxera had yet to be identified
in Marlborough. Fortunately for us, there was a grape-growing gold rush in

Pete Masters when he was foreman at Corbans, 1987

full swing and an acute shortage of vines to plant. Business boomed, as we were selling rootlings at $1.50 with a good margin in each. My diaries and ledgers from that time show, by the day, how many thousands of cuttings we sold to everyone from the Giesens and the Donaldsons (Pegasus Bay), both down in Canterbury, to Alan Brady of Gibbston Valley and Rob Hay at Chard Farm, both in Central Otago, as well as Hermann Seifried in Nelson and pretty much every recognisable name in Marlborough:

- 29,000 Sauvignon Blanc and 10,000 Chardonnay plants for Richard Bowling of Vavasour
- 200 Pinot Noir cuttings for Hunter's
- 300 Cabernet Franc and 100 Merlot for John Forrest
- 200 Pinot Noir for Cloudy Bay, followed five days later by an order for 700 more
- 2,570 Sauvignon Blanc for Matador.

There are hundreds more entries, one after another — some orders as small as fifty vines, some in the thousands, and some in the tens of thousands, with nearly everybody repeat or multiple customers. At one point I even created a map showing all of the vineyards around the valley that were planted using cuttings from our nursery — our fingerprint was found everywhere in Marlborough.

While I am grateful that we did so well, so quickly — especially since it helped pay Vic's school fees, even though she hated being away with a passion and later returned home to attend Marlborough Girls' College — I am especially proud that we were able to create so much opportunity for so many other people who were a part of Mascott. Pete was one of the biggest reasons for the operation's success, as he is one of the hardest-working guys I have ever known. Perhaps the greatest joy of this time was seeing what Mascott was able to do for him. In just those few short years he helped run Mascott, Pete was able to buy a home. He later went on to set up and manage Spy Valley's vineyards, and several other members of his family started contracting businesses of their own.

Pete is but one of many people I can think of, off the top of my head, who never get credit for playing a vital part in Marlborough's rise in New Zealand wine and, eventually, its appearance on the world stage. Growing grapes and making wine is nearly always a gritty, hands-on endeavour completely lacking in any kind of acclaim or adulation. It is tough, it is tiring, and the margins are slim: 99 per cent of people in the wine business struggle to make ends meet. A fraction are lucky enough to have their names on a vineyard or a winery, and most of them probably didn't get their hands dirty along the way. Fewer still make a fortune, even if the perception is that wealthy vintners comprise the rule, not the exception. The only reason that a vineyard or winery ever succeeds is because of someone — or a staff of people — like Pete Masters.

One of the other misconceptions is about what it takes to be a top-class winemaker. Most seem to believe that it is having as many degrees on the wall as you would find in a neurosurgeon's office. In my experience, such degrees are useful for those who wish to break into winemaking at a corporate level — but no one in the wine industry earns greater respect

Paddy Borthwick, our first full-time winemaker at Allan Scott Wines

than those who have been through the mill and gained hands-on experience from a young age. A New Zealand winemaker who fits this description to a T is John Belsham.

Most people know John from his several years at Wairau River Wines, as well as for his own brand, Foxes Island. He was also chairman of the judges for the Air New Zealand Wine Awards for several years. But I know him as the winemaking adviser on the very first vintage of Allan Scott wine in 1990, someone who never hesitated to extend himself or share his ample wisdom. I also reckon I sought his expertise on the first Allan Scott wines out of a kinship of sorts, given that he and I both started in wine by working from very humble beginnings — he in a Bordeaux cellar, me planting sticks at Brancott. (Neither he nor I would probably ever admit it openly, but maybe subconsciously we both feel that we still have something to prove.)

John started out at Hunter's; a young, ambitious, intelligent and intensely serious winemaker already wise beyond his years. He had learned and mastered his trade long before he arrived in Marlborough, though. After leaving school, he was wandering around Europe and eventually landed in Bordeaux, where he would spend five vintages, 1977 through 1981, working in the vineyards and wineries. While Ernie Hunter was the face of the Hunter's brand through the mid-1980s, and of the delicious, trophy-winning wines that each passing year seemed to produce, John was most definitely the wizard behind the curtain.

One thing that John knew from his time in Europe was that most of the bottles that people grab from the supermarket on their way home from work are not crafted at some big, opulent château. Even today, some of the best European wines are made at massive co-operative facilities, where local growers bring their grapes to be crushed and sold off, or to make wines under their own, small labels. John saw that, while Marlborough had no such thing as a co-op winery, it needed one very badly. So just down the road from Hunter's and a stone's throw from the Stoneleigh winery, John set up VinTech, a co-op winery where small- and medium-size growers could

My brother-in-law and Allan Scott Wines vineyard manager Brian Kenny inspecting self-grafted vines

make their wines at his facility and draw on his expertise and experience. (VinTech would become Rapaura Vintners, and grew so quickly that it eventually overtook the Stoneleigh winery on the corner of Jacksons and Rapaura roads — today Matua's winery.) Suddenly, any small grower could have a wine label — something we probably would never have thought we could do before John opened VinTech's doors. Cathy and I, quite happily, were the first customers he signed up.

While John oversaw the early Allan Scott vintages, our first fully employed winemaker was a Roseworthy-trained fellow named Paddy Borthwick, who had been working under John at VinTech. Paddy's thumbprint was on our early wines as much as John's, and what I loved about working with Paddy was his positive, enthusiastic approach to tasks large and small — he was always smiling. He and I worked closely together, and most everything I know today

Our first bottling, at Grove Mill Winery, with Dave Pearce supervising and Cathy manually capping the bottles

about winemaking I learned from him; I like to think I returned the favour, as Paddy gained the confidence over time to single-handedly plant his own vineyard and establish a successful winery in his native Wairarapa.

We were eager to get going with our own wines. Even though we were doing well at contracting and selling cuttings under Mascott, it was only about six months into our new, non-corporate life that Cathy and I realised that we missed the wine side of the business that we had enjoyed so much at Corbans. Because at Corbans I'd had a wine allowance, we had been constantly buying and trying new wines, and learning more and more about varieties, regions, vintage variation and so much more. When I quit Corbans, all of that was suddenly gone, and it left a bigger hole in our lives than we could have anticipated. A certain element of fun and excitement was now absent.

We started making our own wines relatively quickly, but on a small scale. The vines surrounding our house were all contracted to Cloudy Bay, but we were able to siphon off a little bit of juice each year, although nothing commercially viable. By 1990, however, we registered the Allan Scott brand and were able to get some Riesling off the Moorland block, across the street from our house. By this time, we owned the majority of the vineyard, but, to support it financially, each year we were still selling off most of the crop to Seifried, in Nelson. Still, we were able to get enough grapes to produce 1,000 cases of Sauvignon Blanc and a small amount of Riesling, both wines made at VinTech and bottled at Grove Mill. Dave Pearce was on hand to help us make sure that everything went smoothly — our main employees on the bottling line were Cathy, Josh and Sara. Let's just say the kids required a little supervision, given both were still under ten years of age.

Now, any winery owner will tell you that the thing they struggle with most is distribution — finding a company in New Zealand (or several entities abroad) that will hit the streets to sell your wine for you, knocking on restaurant and wine-shop doors. We were incredibly lucky that a fellow named Brent Newell, whom I had worked with at Montana in the 1970s, had set up Eurowine, a distribution company in Wellington. He told me that if I ever made a wine of my own, he wanted to distribute it. He picked up all 1,000 cases of our wine and sold them practically overnight.

All of this happened with the 1990 vintage — our year of establishment as noted on the roadside sign in front of our winery on Jacksons Road. However, much of that period is a blur, even the construction of the building itself. I can't even remember the day or time when we decided to move forward and break ground — we just built it. I do remember that we worked incredibly hard to spare expenses where we could; I even reclaimed the doors and some other elements of the building from a dump near Christchurch. We had to be careful not to fall into the trap that so many others have, building opulent wine-country temples to themselves, then bobbing on a quicksand foundation of debt. The reason why so little of the experience stands out in my mind is that at the same time we were staying true to the advice of Cathy's father, in that we never, ever stood still — primarily with land deals.

In the couple of years leading up to our commencing construction on the winery, we were constantly buying a block, selling another, contracting on this one, flicking on that one. Much of it was subdivided sections of the original Moorland block I had planted when I was with Corbans, although some other pieces were still planted with kiwifruit or apples. In one case, a guy who owned orchards was divesting his assets because of his divorce, so we were able to buy his block, develop it for grapevines, then turn around and sell it off at a profit. It was a complete churn-and-burn cycle in which for every piece of land there was the choice of keeping it and trying to service the debt on it, which was usually impossible, or just turning it around and finding a new owner for it. That is why, before I even realised it, we owned the amount of land we needed to, and could manage it financially, and the builders were working away on the winery.

This isn't something unique to our winery, by any means. All of the time wineries are selling one vineyard in order to buy another, or starting a contract with a new grower as the previous one decides they want to work with a different winery. I'll give you a brief glimpse of how complicated all this can be, using the Moorland vineyard that surrounds the Allan Scott winery today as an example.

Kevin Peterson and I set up a partnership in the mid-1980s to buy that 24-hectare block when Corbans was trying to sell off assets. We then subdivided it into three equal portions of 8 hectares each, and sold off one to afford the rest. Soon after that, the 40-hectare orchard just behind the Moorland estate came up for sale, and Cathy and I purchased and subdivided it into 8-hectare blocks as well — three of which we sold off. Shortly thereafter, Kevin introduced me to Len Evans, the founder of Rothbury Estate in Australia; Rothbury bought one of the blocks, as Evans was keen to expand his reach into New Zealand. Rothbury was about to become part of the Hardys empire, and that company invited us to put our assets in the mix and become part of this large, publicly traded winery. (If we had, today we would be part of Constellation Brands, the largest wine company in the world, which owns Kim Crawford, Nobilo, Monkey Bay, Selaks and Drylands, to name just a few.) I felt that we were too small to be a part of something so big-time, never mind that we were struggling to keep the bank at bay on the blocks we already did own. Over the next several years, we were able to buy back more and more of the subdivided blocks, including the Rothbury section as well as Kevin's pieces. (He was based in Auckland, and was devoting more of his time and efforts to commercial real estate

Our cellar door, made from rammed earth, under construction in 1990

and accounting, his primary businesses.) By 1990, Cathy and I owned most of the property you see around the winery today — all after many years of whirlwind buying, replanting, subdividing, reselling and repurchasing, all the while trying to keep the lenders content.

This is why, to some extent, establishing the winery towards the end of 1990 didn't create a sense of relief or excitement, much less make us feel we had finally, truly made it. It was simply the next, natural step in an otherwise frenzied process — and life! — in which we were trying to keep things in motion and continue to take educated risks in order to grow our business. Who knew if we could keep it going? Certainly not us; the only thing we knew how to do was to try. Success and failure are almost irrelevant, as long as we never sit still.

For the first several years the 'winery' was just a cellar door, not an actual winery. Most of the production was taking place at VinTech, so we were simply lucky that John Belsham had decided to get his operation up and running at precisely the same time as we decided to launch a wine brand of our own. We were lucky, too, to partner with Highfield Estate Winery, which was able to press juice for us at a small, per-litre cost, and truck it in a tanker back down to VinTech. Our winery didn't become production-ready until just before the 1996 vintage. However, it was good that we had started planning for it early on, as the demand for Allan Scott wines kept growing from our inception. The first vintage was 1,000 cases; the second year 2,000 cases; the next year 5,000 cases; the year after 10,000 cases. Highfield also had a bottling line it wanted to sell, so we bought a half-share in that, figuring we would make extra money doing contract bottling for other wineries around Marlborough. Shortly thereafter, though, we were able to buy the whole thing, and bring it down to our winery. We needed it to meet our own rising demand.

In a normal time and place, buying vineyards, building a cellar door, then a winery, then adding in a bottling line would have cost a mind-blowing fortune. But we were extremely lucky to be in the right place at the right time, and to forge strong business alliances and friendships that made all of these things possible in a sensible, logical and affordable sequence of events. I often look at our winery, our vineyards and even our house, and shake my head with wonder at how remarkably fortunate it was that everything fell into place, each piece of the puzzle slotting in after the next. We didn't have investors, nor sometimes much of a clue about what we were doing; we just took a punt, and pressed forward. If we made a misstep, we shrugged it off and worked that much harder as we moved on, rarely looking back.

However, that was the very mindset that almost buried us.

I DIGRESS ...

My tendency to fall asleep in social or business situations has only got worse with age. The trick, I have found, is to avoid times and places where the likelihood of nodding off is that much stronger — and I have help in this regard. Typically, ahead of a long, overseas business trip, Vic, Josh or someone else in the office will email or ring my contacts in advance to make sure no one has planned any late-night meetings or dinners at which I might drift off, as jet lag doesn't ever help my condition. This also means that the distributors, salespeople and sommeliers I am scheduled to meet with are at least forewarned, and so will not feel terribly insulted if I do happen to fall asleep in their presence, particularly if it is only for a brief moment.

Of course, there is no need for such measures if I am on the road with family, but it does sometimes leave them or me with a little explaining to do. One time, when Josh and I were on an extended trip to America, we took a night off from sales meetings to go have dinner somewhere nice. Josh selected a bottle off the wine list, and when the sommelier returned to our table he commenced the usual protocol of presenting the label, followed by removing the foil and uncorking, a few feet away. While he was engaged with all that, I could feel the sensation of sleep beginning to overtake me, but I thought I could fight it off for a while yet.

The sommelier returned to the table and poured a splash of wine into my glass. I swirled the glass, lifted it to my nose and …

Zzzzzz …

I was out cold, my face resting on the rim of some very nice stemware. The sommelier, to his credit, just stood there patiently as if I were taking extra special care to identify and contemplate the aromas wafting into my nostrils. But he could have poured diesel into the glass and I would have been none the wiser.

'Dad!' Josh said sharply, startling me awake.

'Yup, the wine's good!' I immediately said as I shot back to consciousness. The sommelier backpedalled, turned and stepped away from our table, obviously completely confused as to what had just happened.

Because I am so careful about my condition when I am travelling abroad, I am perhaps a bit too lax about it here at home. A few years ago, at the house of John and Jo Stichbury — part-owners of Jackson Estate — dinner came to an abrupt end when I began snoring. Sometimes, though, when I feel as if it's just regular sleep coming on, I can stop whatever it is I am doing and take the nap my body seems to need.

Fairly recently, our UK importer was staying at our house and, when I started to feel a little tired after dinner, I simply stretched out on the long, wooden bench at our kitchen table and slept for an hour or so. Our somewhat baffled business partner moved over to the couch and watched a little TV while I slept; once I awoke, he remarked at how surprised he was that anyone could sleep comfortably on a long, thin plank of wood. Ever since, he has told people, 'That Allan Scott could sleep on barbed wire.' It's probably true.

But, without question, the worst time and place I fell asleep was at the birthday celebration for my old friend Christopher Fielden. He has been in the wine business for decades, partly as an importer in the United Kingdom (and is a longtime champion of our wines), and he has also written several books about wine. Chris decided that he wanted to spend his birthday in New Zealand, the pinnacle of the journey being dinner with me and Cathy at the Hans Herzog Restaurant.

The Hans Herzog winery is unique in Marlborough, in that it didn't produce a single drop of Sauvignon Blanc for many years, and instead made a Bordeaux-style Merlot-Cabernet blend, a Montepulciano, Chardonnay, Viognier, Pinot Noir and Pinot Gris. Most of the wines age for several years before they are released — only when Hans, the Swiss proprietor, feels they are ready. They are among the best — and most expensive — wines in Marlborough. Along with a different approach to wine, Hans and his wife, Therese, also felt that Marlborough needed a top-class restaurant, which they have now owned and operated on their property for many years. With a degustation menu, a beautiful atmosphere, a voluminous wine list spanning myriad regions and vintages, and even a Cuban cigar list, it is arguably the best restaurant in New Zealand, and is certainly unmatched among those situated at wineries. The chef and staff are usually flown in from Switzerland for each busy season, to make sure that no element of service is less than perfect.

In short, Chris was counting on a posh, epic birthday dinner — which he got. What he didn't receive, however, was my full, uninterrupted consciousness.

I simply could not stay awake. What made it all the more embarrassing was that Hans and Therese were there that evening, frequently stopping by our table to chat or see how we were enjoying our meal. And yet no matter what I tried, nothing would keep me awake. Sometimes the sensation is a bit like being drunk, and casual observers start to become worried, or twist their faces into that unmistakable expression that reads, 'What's that guy's problem?'

I tried everything: I took a brief stroll outside; I went to the loo to wash my face with cold water; I took a longer walk outside, around Hans's 11-hectare vineyard. But nothing stops the sleepiness once it starts to set in, no matter how hard I try. Eventually, I fell asleep right at the table.

'FOR GOD'S SAKE, ALLAN!' Christopher screamed. 'PULL YOURSELF TOGETHER!'

The restaurant fell silent. Servers were frozen in their tracks. Every other diner was looking at us, forks or wine glasses suspended in front of their faces. They would have been all the more surprised if they had known Chris personally, as he is incredibly posh and composed. This was more than a bit out of character for him.

But even a suddenly unwound Brit, who had gone off like a hand grenade, wasn't enough to keep me awake. I felt terrible: my dear friend had travelled halfway around the world for dinner with us — the least I could do would be to remain awake. But I had to be taken home, with Cathy remarking to me later that, to the entire restaurant, I looked like a silly, legless drunk.

I suppose the upshot is that Chris now knows to make the restaurant bookings a bit earlier in the evening. And, on the bright side, he most assuredly got a birthday dinner he can't possibly forget.

CHAPTER 9

FOOL ME ONCE, SHAME ON YOU; FOOL ME TWICE, SHAME ON ME

THE SUCCESS OR FAILURE OF A BUSINESS IS NEVER
really as simple as depicted in the movies or as distilled to its basics in news
reports. A single, isolated decision rarely leads to a startling run of success
or a tragic downfall. Fortunes rise and fall as a result of a confluence of
several good or multiple bad decisions — or even a combination of the two,
never mind some elements completely beyond one's control. It's usually in
an unforeseeable manner that seemingly ancient choices and actions start
playing out and suddenly come together for things to blow up for better or
for worse. For us, in the mid-1990s, it was for worse.

In the early 1990s, as Kevin Peterson was bowing out and Pete Masters
and I were shutting down our Mascott nursery business, Cathy and I were
taking over more and more sections of the Moorland vineyard as we began to
grow the Allan Scott brand. Things went smoothly for the first few vintages,
with production of, and demand for, Allan Scott wines rising each year. Only
good things were ahead, including the reclamation of the last big section of
the Moorland vineyard.

Our first export shipment of Sauvignon Blanc being loaded at Lyttelton, 1993

As we were taking it over in 1993, I went to Australia to see the block's owner, Len Evans of Rothbury Estate. While we were enjoying what you might call an elegant drinking session — as you do in Australia, and especially at Len's Hunter Valley property, Loggerheads — he invited the Allan Scott winery to participate in the share float that would combine Rothbury and Hardys into a publicly traded company. As mentioned previously, I declined, but I will also be the first to admit that the afternoon at Len's had given me some pretty wild ideas about what might be possible for the Allan Scott brand, as well as for our bank balances.

While this particular opportunity wasn't quite right for us, the notion of taking Allan Scott public in some shape or form was an incredibly exciting prospect, and it was an idea I couldn't shake off. This was especially so because we were basically doubling the size of our production each year, and so going public seemed a reasonable proposition somewhere down the track.

On my way back home, in the airport, I ran into Terry Shagin, the founder of Regal Salmon Limited. Although his primary base of knowledge and experience was salmon farming in the Marlborough Sounds, he was more than familiar with the wine business. Terry and I had met several times before, as he was an investor in Cellier Le Brun, the winery of my close friend Daniel Le Brun. The chance encounter seemed like kismet.

'I'm thinking of taking Cellier Le Brun public,' he told me. 'Maybe you want to come in on the deal?'

You can imagine how I felt. It was like getting a trial for the All Blacks, and feeling I wasn't quite up to the challenge, then on the way home being asked to be in the starting XV for Canterbury — no shame in that whatsoever, and more befitting my skills and experience. I had got a taste of the big-time, and perhaps it was just a matter of finding the right place for me in it, I surmised. This felt like it could be the move we were waiting for, the best part being that Cathy and I knew all of the other players on the team. With Rothbury and Hardys, there was considerable fear of the unknown, given how many other, larger players were in on the proceedings. But not in this particular scenario.

Over weeks and weeks of meetings, each one bringing in new investor faces, strategists, advisers and hangers-on, the deal started to take shape. A $16 million company called Appellation would be created, its operating units being Allan Scott, Cellier Le Brun, Morton Estate and Regal Salmon. At the time, Morton Estate was owned by Wolf Blass, which was keen to sell it; for the entire deal to come together, Appellation needed a bigger winery in the mix, and Morton satisfied that requirement. Despite the number of players involved (including, just representing the Allan Scott portion, Westpac Bank and Prudential Insurance), every piece of the puzzle managed to come together exactly when and where it was needed.

Today, I have to admit, the notion of even large wine companies as publicly traded entities seems a bit crazy to me. This is because in winemaking countless factors are beyond the companies' control — the weather, volatile international currency markets, even more volatile fuel and transportation

Displaying our wares at the Marlborough Food and Wine Festival, 1993

costs, thin margins, seemingly incalculable expansion and growth costs (vineyards and grapes are insanely expensive), and so on. Knowing all this, and with 20–20 hindsight today, the entire idea of Appellation was completely absurd because of the bad timing and the somewhat strange bedfellows. A salmon farm teamed up with wineries? It just didn't make sense.

It certainly didn't to Cathy.

'If this is the right thing to be doing,' she said to me, 'shouldn't we be celebrating with a bottle of Champagne?'

That's the sentence that opened the first chapter of this book. As I wrote there, not only was this the turning point for us as a family and as a business but it was also the moment that proved that Cathy's instincts are nearly always spot-on. There we were in 1993, seated at our kitchen table and surrounded by piles of documents, Cathy's sixth sense telling us exactly what we needed to know. But for some reason we thought, sod it, and signed the Memorandum of Understanding to participate in the Appellation launch and share float.

I wouldn't go as far as to say that our worst fears were realised, slowly or immediately, because everything about this was uncharted territory. What we began experiencing, however, was the classic scenario you always hear about immediately after a company's fortunes turn to custard, when people say, 'Our first warning should have been that the business was too complex for anyone to explain it properly — that should have been our signal to tuck tail and run.' We felt ambivalent at best, and grew more concerned with each passing day. And then we had our first meeting with all of the key players.

Nothing felt right about it. The body language between several people in the room was all wrong, as if a couple of them were in on some secret that the rest of us weren't. So we asked our lawyer, David Dew (who has done the legal work for nearly every winery of note in Marlborough since the very beginning), to arrange a separate meeting between us and Terry Shagin, at which we could raise our concerns. Terry assured us that everything was fine. Two days later, things were anything but.

We learned that the stock of Regal had been overvalued wildly, and its share price tumbled instantly. Financially, Regal was an anchor encased in a block of cement, sinking to the bottom of the Marlborough Sounds. The other end of the chain was latched to our ankles. Immediately, we knew that we would have to take any and every legal measure available to break free of Appellation.

Unfortunately, even though the deal had yet to be completed, the Memorandum of Understanding we had signed was more or less watertight – there wasn't a single linguistic loophole through which we could make a legal escape. But once we had signalled to all of the other parties that we wanted out, and had taken the extra step of hiring a forensic accountant named John Buchanan (recommended to us by Kevin Peterson) to help unwind everything, step by step, Appellation quickly shifted from being a collection of small, family companies all content to play together in the same sandbox, to a knockdown, drag-out battle royal.

Each board meeting in Wellington or Auckland was heated and emotional. Worse, because there was a fair amount of cash in the pool, not to mention reasonably good assets (meaning our winery, Morton Estate and Le Brun, never mind the salmon farm), the vultures started circling. All of those semi-interested advisers and hangers-on, who had seemed like background supporting characters in the story as everyone came together, all of a sudden were right in the thick of it, trying to get their cut, since they would never get the chance to sell their shares and get their cash out after the float. We were fending them off with one hand, while trying to gather and reclaim every piece that was ours.

As things were reaching their boiling point, with backstabbing seemingly becoming the norm, one interested party came in underneath and tried to undermine everything by talking separately to the Le Bruns. The fellow was in Daniel and Adele's living room, calmly making his pitch to them.

'If you want to save what you have, you've got to get to Daniel's house and sort things out — *now*,' a mutual friend in the know said to me over the telephone that evening, no ambiguity whatsoever in his tone of voice.

I drove as quickly as I could to Daniel and Adele's house, full of rage and ready for fisticuffs if necessary. I'm sure my face was beet-red as I screamed at the guy who had been trying to drive a wedge between us and the Le Bruns. All the while, poor Adele wore an expression on her face that said she knew she would need to clean blood off her carpet at some point that evening. Thankfully, fists didn't fly and the guy left the scene — and Marlborough — empty-handed.

Things calmed down considerably after that, mostly because everyone knew where they stood. The house of cards had fallen, and everyone agreed that the family of companies that had come together would be happiest on their own. Appellation was untangled bit by bit, slowly and peacefully over the next six months. Our situation could only improve from there, but we still had many more lessons to learn about getting too comfortable, too quickly.

They say that victims of trauma are unable to process mentally what they are experiencing in the moment, and for months or even years after they are unable to describe the sequence of events fully. In some ways, I know how they feel. The Appellation experiment didn't feel particularly bad or even abnormal while we were going through it, but as time goes on, and each time I think back to it, I realise how close we were to utter disaster. Cathy and I were incredibly lucky to save what we had worked so hard to build — all of it could have been gone the instant we signed that one document.

At least the essence of this started to sink in as our accountant helped us restore all of our finances through a complicated series of transactions. In a sense, we were starting over, as the Appellation deal had required us to sever

A family day out in Christchurch: left to right, Sara, Cathy, Josh and Vic, 1994

most of our previous business relationships. We even had to go back to our bank, almost as if we were strangers whom they had never met previously, and re-pitch and re-present our entire business as a credible venture so they would work with us again on basic banking and loan services. It was even mildly embarrassing, almost like a teenager who's broken things off with his girlfriend, and then has to sit her down a year later and explain why we he was such an idiot to have left her for a slightly prettier woman who had done an incredible job of hiding her true ill temper.

In some sense, John Buchanan and his business partner, Steve Hotchin, weren't just our accountants: they were our knights in shining armour. Having untangled an enormously complicated mess on our behalf, they were the the most obvious people to turn to for help in figuring out what to do next with Allan Scott. We still had a solid brand with more than enough demand for our wines, never mind some good vineyards and a cellar door that was gaining more visitors each week, month and year. But we were suddenly short on cash after the Appellation mess, and we had no real idea how we could expand the business and regain our momentum. The excitement and enthusiasm for Marlborough wine was only growing, as around this time Cloudy Bay was already turning heads worldwide — that little country in the South Pacific was making Sauvignon Blanc that tasted better than Sancerre. Not to abuse a metaphor, but the train would soon be leaving the station, and we knew we had to get back on it. Fortunately, John had an idea.

'Steve and I have been thinking about getting into the wine business,' John told me and Cathy. We found this a bit strange, at first, that two accountants who had just spent months untangling a god-awful mess would want to dive right back into the inherent silliness that is the wine industry. But their proposal made sense. 'We'll keep our accounting practice, you keep the Allan Scott business. Together, we'll go into a partnership on new vineyards that Steve and I will invest in personally. You can use the fruit to supply Allan Scott, and we'll start a new brand, together, that will take some of the grapes – the rest we'll sell off to other wineries.'

It was perfectly sensible — brilliant, even, in its simplicity. And if Cathy and I craved anything in the business at this point, indeed it was simple, straightforward practices. The only question would be what to name the new venture. We didn't have to think hard about it at all: Mount Riley.

Late in my tenure at Corbans, the company's general manager, Kevin Peterson, and I had privately made a Chardonnay we called Moorland Estate, and we cocked it up pretty badly. We sent the wine up to Michael Brajkovich at Kumeu River in Auckland, who finished it off for us — and did a rather cracking job of it. Unfortunately, we learned after a couple years that Montana owned the trademark on the Moorland name, so we changed the name of the brand to Mount Riley. After Kevin had drifted away from wine to focus on other things, Cathy and I retained the Mount Riley brand, which we had already had registered. So now there was really no work to do: we simply had to draft agreements as to what the new partnership would look like. John and Steve would each own one-third of Mount Riley, and Cathy and I would own the other third.

Immediately, and with a rekindled relationship with our bank, we set about buying vineyards. It was easy, because John and Steve had no problems whatsoever borrowing or raising money — it was all familiar territory for them, so any viticultural wish quickly came true.

First we acquired a very good block of Chardonnay vines at the intersection of Old Renwick and St Leonards roads, which had previously been owned by a grower for Villa Maria. Next was a property close to Renwick, right along the Wairau River, which we bought from Richie Dillon, one of the original settler families of the Waihopai Valley. It was a labour of love developing that block, as the section close to the river needed to be dug up and drained. But we put our hearts into it from start to finish, ripping out all of the existing vegetation, and cultivating, irrigating and planting. It is still, I think, one of the more beautiful vineyards in Marlborough, with the imposing Mount Riley itself just behind it. There was another block I wasn't particularly fond of — right near the old lucerne mill off Old Renwick Road — since I believed

The Seventeen Valley Vineyard at the southern entrance to Blenheim

it was a little too exposed and would be more susceptible to frost than our other properties. But John was quite keen on that one, and he certainly deserved a say, so we scooped up that property as well.

The real gem, however, was the Seventeen Valley Vineyard, at the opposite end of Marlborough, along the coast near the road to Seddon. In my opinion, it remains one of the best spots in Marlborough — something I began to learn as far back as the late 1970s. When I worked for Montana, the guy who owned that farm was keen on growing grapes. He got in touch with me and told me that he wanted to plant vines, but I thought the land was a bit too far away from everyone and everything — and probably too cold.

'No, quite the opposite,' the owner said to me. 'It's actually quite warm here. This land is very different from everything else around here. All my plants come up early and last longer into autumn.'

I didn't believe him, but I put a weather station on the property to get some data anyway — and it turned out that he was right. The land was averaging five full degrees warmer than anywhere else on the Wairau Plain. I did a little more research and found that the land had once been the site of gardens for the Maori, the original settlers of the land. They knew the land was warm. Several years later, I met a fellow who told me that, when he was a child, he and his friends would ride their bikes down the road from Seddon every day for school — especially in winter, they would stop right at that spot to warm up before they pedalled on. They would be freezing, their knuckles on the handlebars pure white, and then they would be hit with an intense burst of warm air as they entered that pocket. All this is a roundabout way of saying that, if anyone were to plant vines on that piece of land, they would find a longer, more even ripening season than anywhere else in Marlborough — and, likely, superior wine quality. This is why it was amazing to me that, all the way up to the mid-1990s — two full decades after I had first looked at the property — no one had planted it with grapevines.

It turned out that the original owner I'd met had eventually lost interest in planting grapes. He sold the land to another farmer and, before he died, told the buyer that I had conducted some research on the land. When the new owner was ready to sell the property, around late 1994, he rang me and asked whether I would be interested in buying and planting the land. I told John and Steve everything I knew about the property, and we didn't hesitate. We bought and established the land, and actually started with Italian varieties such as Barbera and Montepulciano, along with Pinot Noir, since the data suggested that this small slice of Marlborough is as warm as Tuscany. But, almost immediately, by far the best results could be seen with the Pinot Noir.

Our business relationship with John and Steve felt perfect, because, thanks to them, we were able to put the Appellation mess into the rearview mirror incredibly quickly, and before we knew it we had re-established ourselves. We didn't have to worry about money, grape supply or winemaking, since we were able to maintain our ties to Highfield, where we did our pressing, as well as VinTech, where the Allan Scott and Mount Riley wines were made.

In fact, Mount Riley proved so successful right out of the gates that the extra income serviced our debt on the new property purchases easily, with plenty left over. Our distributor in Wellington was actually getting a bit upset with us, because restaurants and wine shops were marketing Mount Riley as 'the cheaper Allan Scott', which started to hurt our sales a bit. To be honest, though, the label was so successful that we didn't really care all that much that Mount Riley was the tail wagging the dog.

John Buchanan in England, 1997

More importantly, though, John and Steve, we felt, were the first partners we had had who truly understood our family, as well as its connection to our business and what we wanted to achieve with it. I reckon that's part of their job — in looking through years of our accounting records, the numbers and transactions all told our story of where we started, where we were and where we wanted to go. Things went swimmingly, and we all became close friends. As I was looking back through old photographs for this book, I stumbled across a set from a trip to Europe to visit several regions and wineries — John and I are pictured in several, laughing and smiling as if the party couldn't possibly end.

The needle on the record skipped, however, with the 1995 vintage. If you have ever read any books about Marlborough's wine history, you'll know that they all mention the horror that was the harvest in 1995. Every wine region has a shocker that is still discussed as if it were a natural disaster on a par with the explosion of Krakatoa, the Boxing Day tsunami and the Great Depression, all in one. (Vintners do have a tendency to dramatise a bit — a quality we share all around the world.) Bordeaux has seen some doozies, although the one lamented most often is probably 1960; for the Rhône, the floods of 2002 made for some awfully thin, flavourless wines; back to back, 1982 and 1983 were rainy stinkers in Napa that California winemakers claim they are still recovering from; but for New Zealand the nadir was unquestionably 1995.

There were only about two dozen Marlborough wineries at the time, but not one in the industry could escape the impact of a natural disaster several thousand kilometres away: the 1994 secondary eruption of Mount Pinatubo in the Philippines. This volcano had been dormant for about 400 years, up until a massive, violent reawakening in 1991 that covered several surrounding kilometres with a thick layer of lava and ash, killed nearly 200 people, displaced roughly 1 million others and actually cooled global temperatures by about two degrees. But it was the mountain's late-1994 encore performance that pushed a cloud of ash high into the atmosphere — one that eventually drifted over New Zealand.

What followed were weeks and weeks of cool weather and rain, much of it landing on Marlborough just before and during harvest. Although Pinatubo has been quiet ever since, nowadays the industry could handle a sustained stretch of cool, rainy weather caused by any natural event for two primary reasons: first, we have the equipment, machinery and tank space to harvest quickly and efficiently if we need to, which no one had in 1995; second, modern winemaking relies heavily on managing the grape crop much more carefully, whereas up to about 2000 the standard practice was to grow as many grapes as possible. Modern viticulture is the only type of farming I am aware of in which the goal isn't to grow as much of a crop as you possibly can, but to maintain a balanced amount of grapes on each and every vine, so that all of the fruit ripens steadily and consistently, ready for picking at the end of the season.

This is a big part of why 1995 was such a disaster. The season had been warm and dry up to the arrival of the Pinatubo ash cloud, so all of the vines were carrying relatively heavy crops that had yet to ripen fully. Most of the valley was planted with young Sauvignon Blanc vines that were incredibly vigorous, and this was long before it became standard practice to go through the vineyards and snip off grape clusters so that each vine can fully ripen its fruit by autumn. When the rains set in, all of the grapes on the vines began swelling with water. Then they started to split and rot, and become infected with *Botrytis* — a fungus that is a necessary ingredient for the production of sweet dessert wines such as Sauternes and late-harvest Riesling, but is the sworn enemy in the production of dry table wines. It is an absolute quality-killer.

The cool weather and rain arrived and remained as steady and monotonous as watching a *Coronation Street* marathon. (Although, I have to confess, that British soap opera has long been a guilty pleasure of mine.) Everything else conspired to go wrong as a result: we didn't have enough harvesting machinery and staff in Marlborough to bring the grapes in off the vines quickly (and who wants to work in the cold, pouring rain anyway?); there weren't even enough trucks to cart the grapes from the vineyards to the wineries for crushing and pressing; and no winery had enough tank space to hold the massive loads of rain-swollen grapes coming in all at once, when and if it was actually possible to arrange for a harvester and a truck.

Up to that point, for two decades everyone had been thinking solely about planting vineyards and growing grapes. No one had thought about investing in wineries that were large enough to handle all of that fruit. Except, perhaps, for John Belsham at VinTech. Suddenly he was very popular, as everyone needed to get their grapes pressed and the juice into his tanks. He was the only one with extra capacity heading into the harvest, but every one of his large, shiny tanks was full of juice very quickly.

Prior to 1995, the only wet season Marlborough had seen was 1978, when the industry was still in its infancy. I can still remember John Marris ordering us to pull all of the harvesters up and down Montana's rows with bulldozers in an utter fit of desperation to get the grapes off the vines. The improvisation didn't get quite so ridiculous in 1995, but there was plenty of it taking place. Many people stored their wine in tanks at dairy factories up and down New

Zealand, since the one stroke of luck was that it wasn't the season for milking cows and making cheese. Marris, by the way, owned one of the only four-wheel-drive harvesters in Marlborough at the time, and was able to charge a premium to anyone desperate to pick and salvage what was left of their crop.

If you actually did have tank and winery space organised, as we had reserved for us at VinTech, you could see how terrible the quality was the instant the truck dropped off a load of grapes. One of our growers, I remember, came up to the winery and used a sledgehammer to bang every strainer-post; each time he did, a layer of rotten grapes, 8 centimetres thick, would rain out onto the ground. It was as disgusting as it was disheartening.

Oddly enough, some of the wines that came out of 1995 didn't taste as terrible as everyone expected them to, and the market demand for Marlborough Sauvignon Blanc was starting to reach a fever-pitch at home as well as around the world. The issue, simply, was that Marlborough's wine industry was too immature and inexperienced to be prepared for such an adverse season. That might sound a bit strange considering that, by this time, grape-growing and winemaking had been chugging along relatively smoothly — even with the 1986 vine-pull — for two decades. But such is the nature of winegrowing that 'experience' is a very relative term. However, Cathy and I knew we couldn't afford to get caught out again, struggling to find a harvester or tank space in the face of sustained inclement weather or some other unforeseen event. So we decided we needed our own winery for Allan Scott and Mount Riley, no matter the cost.

After harvest and ahead of the 1996 vintage, we started expanding our cellar door in the Moorland vineyard to include a winery with our own tanks and barrel storage. (We would add a press only in 1997, so for the 1996 vintage we bought an old, 10,000-litre dairy tanker. We could press the juice directly into it, up at the Highfield winery, then drive the juice down to our winery for fermentation, finishing and bottling.) We couldn't rely on the bank for every last capital investment, so we needed to get a little scrappy and stretch our dollar with some intelligence.

ABOVE LEFT: The first grapes being processed at our present site.
ABOVE RIGHT: Cellar hand Craig Murphy, me, an unidentified team member and Paddy Borthwick.

One particular thing that 1995 taught us was that we were in desperate need of a truck to get grapes from the vineyards to the winery. We found an old International truck that to that point had been used for carting around recently harvested onions. We had to do some work on it to make the cargo area watertight, but we were able to use that truck for several more years. We also needed a harvester, and, as luck would have it, I had stayed in touch with a Corbans grower in Tolaga Bay, north of Gisborne, to whom Corbans had sold an extra harvester when it acquired Cooks. That area had been hit by Cyclone Bola in 1988, causing about $235 million of damage (in today's dollars) and wiping out most of the area's vineyards. Almost everyone who had been growing grapes there opted to give up on them and switched to other crops; as a result, the harvester was just sitting up there, unused. I flew up and asked the owner whether I could buy it and two gondolas for $30,000 — an absolute bargain considering that a new harvester can cost half a million or more. The guy was elated to get rid of the thing, so we brought it down to Marlborough and fixed it up. Even though it was a relatively

Our first harvester was an early-model, US-built Chisolm Ryder.

early, American-made harvester with no real bells and whistles, it served us well for several years thereafter, since we almost completely rebuilt it with stainless-steel parts and new fans.

Before I knew it, I looked around and we were a standalone, fully functional, independent winery right in the heart of Marlborough. We weren't sure how we had done it, but, after the Appellation mess and the disastrous 1995 harvest, we had recovered fully — even come out much stronger. While we could pat ourselves on the back for the turnaround, it was also clear that we couldn't have done it without our Mount Riley partners. Thanks to them, the Allan Scott brand was able to get the grapes it needed to survive and expand, and we generated far more cashflow off the Mount Riley brand than any of us had anticipated. We were firmly in the black, sitting pretty.

However, we would soon come to believe that all along our partners had needed us as much as we had needed them.

Enjoying a sunset with Cathy at Sarasota, Florida, in 1998. We had been invited to bring our wines to the famous Sarasota Stone Crab Festival.

I know I have harped on about this already, but I can't emphasise enough that Cathy has a better eye for detail and is a better judge of character than almost anyone I have ever met. One day in early 1997, she was reviewing the books, and she couldn't quite understand why, if both Allan Scott and Mount Riley were performing so well, our accounts weren't as flush with cash as we thought they would be. She went over the books again and again, almost obsessively, and she still couldn't figure out where the money was going.

John and Steve, as accountants and as people, were very different from each other, but they had quite complementary personalities. John was more personable and engaging, while Steve was the shy, more meticulous and serious one. He also kept incredibly thorough, detailed records, and that is where Cathy started to find the missing pieces of the puzzle.

To this day, I can't say who was in the right, much less who was clear about their understanding of the partnership in terms of who earned what amounts and why for their roles in the business. One thing I will say: John is one of the most intelligent people I have met. That is what I admired about him. He was smarter than everyone else in the unwinding of the Appellation partnership, truly saving our hides; he was the smartest person in the Mount Riley collaboration. It is also why Cathy and I couldn't now come to a concession with John and Steve on a revision of the Mount Riley partnership and the percentage they were being afforded as the accountants for the enterprise. In truth, we didn't really try, because we knew that we had received yet another clear signal that we were best off operating on our own. Lesson learned.

Sure, there were heated, emotional discussions as the partnership started to unravel, but they really didn't have anything to do with money or land, even if that's what everyone was arguing about on the surface. The partnership was structured in black and white: John and Steve each had

Passing through Detroit, 1998

235

Attending a charity wine-tasting in Santa Monica, California, in 1999

one-third ownership, so it was their say on absolutely everything. There was really nothing Cathy and I could do when they exercised their right to split off and establish Mount Riley as their own enterprise. We went our separate ways relatively peacefully.

I probably kicked and hollered most about the Seventeen Valley property as we handed it over to them, since I had put so much into it. I sometimes wonder if they wanted it simply because they knew I had hoped to keep it. But I don't miss it now, and I wouldn't take it back even if it was offered to us, since it is 22 kilometres from our winery. Today I think less about the wine quality we used to get from the land and more about the pain in the ass it was sending people and machinery down there to work all the time. To me, the saddest aspect of the falling out was that I knew I was losing a friend. (About a year later, John and Steve went their separate ways as well; John owns and operates Mount Riley on his own, and has done a most impressive job with it.)

I still see John now and again, and we wave hello or exchange pleasantries when we run into each other, but that's about it. For some time, it did make my blood pressure rise a bit whenever I'd drive by a vineyard marked with a Mount Riley road sign. Now, however, I don't let it bother me; in fact, I am quite pleased that there is yet another high-profile Marlborough wine brand that bears my thumbprint. But also, I remind myself that, from the very beginning of the partnership, we were careful to protect what was ours, first and foremost. While losing our third of the partnership was a setback, I can't ignore the fact that the Mount Riley experience positioned us for long-term success. If not for that, we would have had a much more difficult time establishing our own, self-sustaining winery. From that point to today, Allan Scott has been a truly independent, family winery. To signal that, we eventually changed the name of our winery from Allan Scott Wines to Allan Scott Family Winemakers.

I DIGRESS ...

Ever wonder about the gold-, silver- and bronze-medal stickers you sometimes see affixed to wine bottles? The practice of awarding honours to wines was once a bright spot of our nascent industry — healthy competition and a venue for the exchange of information and ideas. Today, however, wine shows are all about marketing, and lack their original jovial spirit. Confirmation of this was a long time coming, although I am probably the last person anyone would have expected to be right in the middle of our biggest competition's darkest hour.

There are about a dozen annual wine competitions in New Zealand. They include the Royal Easter Show, the Romeo Bragato Awards and the Liquorland Top 100, as well as the daddy of them all, the Air New Zealand Wine Awards. All of them follow the same basic set of procedures. Wineries submit their newly released Sauvignon Blancs, Pinot Noirs, Chardonnays and other wines to the competition. An assembled panel of judges — mostly winemakers, but also sometimes distributors, journalists and other invited guests — taste the wines blind and score them from 1 to 20 points. When the scores are combined, wines earn a gold, silver or bronze medal (or do not accumulate enough points to merit an award). The gold-medal winners in each category are then tasted blind, again, to determine which one is the best in class and lands the trophy.

Now, I should pause for a moment and set straight two things, both of which will make me sound like a terrible hypocrite. First, I hate wine shows even though we enter Allan Scott wines into several of these competitions each year; we do it mostly to get a sense of how we match up to other wineries, and don't use the accolades for aggressive marketing purposes. Second, I tend to eschew attention, even though the situation I am about to recount involves me leaping into a bright media spotlight, in which I didn't belong.

However, when controversy overshadowed the Air New Zealand Wine Awards in 2006, I felt it was my duty to stand up for the honest, hardworking people in and connected to the wine industry, who, I believed, had been unfairly vilified. I can't say that anyone came out looking better, as my actions and comments only prolonged a most uncomfortable situation regarding the integrity and public perception of New Zealand winemakers. But perhaps I would do it again, in part because I remember a gentler time when wine shows were driven by purer intentions that better served New Zealand wine as a whole.

When the industry was still in its relative adolescence, wine shows were mostly an excuse for everyone to get together for a big piss-up. Sure, we would all bask in the temporary glow of having earned a medal or two, but we also used the gatherings to share experiences, best practices and ideas about the wines we were making at the moment, as well as the ones we hoped to be able to produce in the future. Most importantly, we all let loose together, united in purpose and ambition.

In the early days, the show was known as the New Zealand Wine Awards, sponsored by the Tourist Hotel Corporation and held at the Chateau Tongariro Hotel, near Lake Taupo. It was the event of the year, a multi-day extravaganza at the crown jewel of tourist hotspots, with everyone in the industry assembled for days of shooting pool, swimming, skiing — you name it — followed by nights of drinking and dancing. I'll never forget one time when a judge, Sir Don Beaven (the famous diabetes researcher from Christchurch School of Medicine), was leaving on the train at about 1 am;

he began doing the wobbly farewell rounds, saying goodbye and shaking hands with the men and kissing the ladies. Bob Campbell, New Zealand's foremost wine critic, walked up and extended his hand. After hours — days, actually — of non-stop imbibing, however, Don simply got confused as he bade farewell to everyone and laid a big, juicy wet one on Bob ... who wore the most stunned expression of any man I have ever seen.

Today, the shows are as brief as they are serious, particularly because several wineries have learned that accumulating medals and trophies can give a measurable boost to wine sales. The unfortunate aspect to this is that great wines and award-winning wines can be mutually exclusive. Winemakers have realised, over consecutive calendar years packed with competitions, that the best-quality wines are quite often overlooked in the wine-show format. Instead, as the judges swirl, sniff, sip and spit more than 100 tastings on each day of the competition, it's wines with elevated levels of sugar, alcohol or both, that tend to stand out and, in turn, win the medals. This state of affairs seems to have become widely accepted (in part because top-quality wines often win medals and trophies, too), especially as the competition shifted from a days-long party to a straightforward marketing exercise.

The limitations of the awards and the compromises being made became all the more apparent in 2006, after *Cuisine*'s wine critic Michael Cooper presided over the magazine's annual ratings of newly released Sauvignon Blancs. He discovered that the 2006 Wither Hills Marlborough Sauvignon Blanc, which the magazine had rated five stars out of five, was different from the wine of the same name available to the general public in grocery stores and wine shops. The former was a run of about 2,000 cases, while the latter was a run of more than 100,000 cases. This is not to say that the widely available wine was bad — Cooper later said that he would have rated it four stars out of five. The issue was simply that the wines were labelled as one and the same, yet they were chemically different as a result of comprising distinct lots of Sauvignon Blanc grapes grown across the winery's array of estate vineyards and growers. Things should have cooled off from there, but it was discovered soon after that the small-production Wither Hills wine had been entered into several other competitions, including the Air New Zealand Awards, where it had won a silver medal.

I knew none of this, however, until I received a text message from a *Wine Spectator* editor,* asking me whether I was aware of the situation, about which he had received a tip. I didn't give the matter any more thought until the story began spreading further and wider a couple of days later, largely due to a *Weekend Herald* story about Cooper's discovery. Soon after that, I received a call from Patrick Gower at *The New Zealand Herald*.

'What do you think about all this?' he asked me.

'I don't know too much about it yet,' I said, 'and generally with these sorts of things, it's best to refer it to the winemakers.' Since I'm not one by trade, I suggested he ring a few to get their thoughts.

'I've been in contact with them, but no one is prepared to comment,' Patrick said, and he then went on to describe what the *Weekend Herald* had reported: specifically that there were two different Wither Hills Sauvignon Blancs, but they were labelled identically. 'Is this a common practice?'

'No, not really,' I said. 'We all suspect that things like this happen, but nothing's ever really come to light.'

'Are you prepared to comment?'

'No,' I said. 'But let me ring a few people and I'll get back to you at the end of the day. Maybe we can make a collective response.'

I called a few winemaker and proprietor friends around Marlborough, and all of them suggested I let sleeping dogs lie. I didn't quite agree with that, but I rang Patrick back and told him that no one was prepared to comment.

'Have you spoken with Michael Cooper?' he asked me.

'No, I rarely speak to him. I know him, of course, but we don't talk regularly by any means.'

'He's pretty upset about it all,' Patrick said. 'He's receiving threatening messages, and God knows what else.'

I was stunned. Threats over a wine competition? It seemed beyond absurd.

'Why don't I give you his number?' Patrick said. 'Talk to him, and if you want to ring me back afterwards, feel free to do so.'

Michael's line rang and rang and rang, but there was no answer. I made several more attempts, and eventually his wife answered; she had been

---

* Eric Arnold, who helped me write this book.

screening the calls. I told her who I was, and Michael came to the phone, and poured his heart out. He was devastated. He had done what he felt was right — and was his responsibility — as New Zealand's leading consumer advocate in wine, but no one had thanked him for being a whistleblower. Instead, he had been targeted viciously — a response I could not comprehend.

But then I remembered the first time we had won a gold medal for our Allan Scott Marlborough Riesling, around 1991 or 1992. We were incredibly excited, as it was our first accolade. But almost immediately afterwards I received a telephone call from Philip Gregan, the head of New Zealand Winegrowers, who told me that he had received an anonymous complaint, accusing us of having brought in a wine from somewhere else and put our label on it — that the gold-medal Riesling wasn't from our vineyard. I told him that if someone wanted to make such an accusation, they would need to front up — but he wouldn't tell me the source of the claim. Either way, I told Philip the truth: that, of course, the wine had come from our bloody vineyard, and we were thrilled to have been recognised for our achievement. That was the end of it, but this new incident a decade and a half later brought all those dark feelings to the surface again. I hate seeing honest work punished, and I felt insulted and ashamed that my colleagues were behaving in such a manner, whoever they were.

I told Michael Cooper that what he discovered wasn't a common practice, as far as I knew, but that everyone had heard rumours that such things happened occasionally. That didn't make them acceptable though, so those who had been caught should be held to account, I affirmed.

'I support you,' I said, as I hung up the phone.

Patrick Gower rang me back a short while later and asked again if I had any comment. I had plenty for him, and, while I don't regret some of my more incendiary remarks on the record, I might have been a touch more cautious with my words had I known they would wind up on the front page of the *Herald* the next morning. The only thing I hoped for and expected was that someone would raise their hand, take responsibility and promise that measures would be put in place to ensure something like this would never happen again — for the sake of preserving the reputation of all New Zealand wineries.

After the story ran, I spoke with a few other proprietors, who told me that they agreed with my stance, but that it was time to remain quiet and let it go. That's what I did from then on, but the story now had legs; it even resulted in an investigation by New Zealand Winegrowers. No evidence of malicious wrongdoing was reported, but everyone involved went on record as saying that there was no excuse, under any circumstances, for a winery to release two different blends bearing the same label. By week's end, Wither Hills had forfeited the awards accumulated by both of the Sauvignon Blanc blends submitted to all competitions, and the Air New Zealand Wine Awards underwent several personnel and format changes.

I won't recount the ensuing coverage, as it didn't do any favours for anyone involved — including me. The longer the story dragged on, the more damaging were the things everyone said on the record about themselves, their colleagues and friends across the industry. In truth, it's tough for anyone to know how to handle media pressure, especially us winemakers and grape-growers, who spend most of our time working with organisms that don't ask questions and behave somewhat predictably each year. Under pressure, it is also very easy to forget that the media will move on the instant they find someone new to scrutinise. That's exactly what they did.

It all serves as a reminder of just what a typhoon-in-a-water-glass the 2006 Air New Zealand Wine Awards were — and that every winery is at its best when the proprietors concern themselves with their own affairs solely, and try to make the best wine possible — nothing more. When we all remain true to this, Marlborough, collectively, makes some of the best wines in the world.

Nonetheless, it is a shame that our wine shows are no longer about everyone getting together and partying until dawn for several days straight, as we used to. But I am hopeful we will see such an era again — and perhaps to get back there one day we all needed to hit rock bottom, together, in 2006.

CHAPTER 10

CONTINUING THE LEGACY

FOR THE PAST TWO DECADES, ALLAN SCOTT HAS
grown steadily and consistently, both as a brand and as a winery. In 2000
we bought our largest property, a 40-hectare apple orchard on Old Renwick
Road a couple of kilometres from the winery, and planted it with Sauvignon
Blanc, Pinot Noir, Chardonnay and Riesling. A few years later we were
able to purchase the adjacent vineyards behind our house, as well as one of
our grower's blocks around the corner, a kilometre or so away along Old
Renwick Road. A few winemakers have come and gone from our cellar
over the years, each possessing different strengths and weaknesses with
specific grape varieties or in general, yet all the while we have maintained
a consistent and reliable house style across our range of single-vineyard,
sparkling, Marlborough and Central Otago wines — no easy feat when you
started at 1,000 cases and grew quickly to 120,000 cases, as the tally stands
today.

While those numbers convey that we have done something right, to me
they are nothing compared to seeing the same faces, from near and far, at

247

Our winery and brewery are now clearly signposted.

our cellar door and restaurant each month and year. And with each week it seems that there is another email, telephone call or visit from someone who has discovered an Allan Scott wine in a New Zealand restaurant or supermarket, or in a wine shop or restaurant in Australia, Canada, America, Ireland, England, Scotland, Japan or Vietnam.

The main reason people around the world like and trust our brand, apart from what's inside the bottle, is simply because we eventually learned from our mistakes of the mid- to late-1990s. We stopped trying to be something other than what we are, which is a winery — nothing more or less. We also stopped trying to do too much, and instead maintained our focus on, and sought improvements in, the few basic things we already knew how to do well. It sounds trite, but in wine — as with so many other things in life — there is no point in becoming consumed with what is happening across the region or even across the road. Primarily, we avoid such distractions by

Josh, Victoria, Cathy, me and Sara, 2015

always remembering why we concentrate our efforts and work as hard as we do in the first place: for our family.

The Allan Scott winery wouldn't have survived without a commitment to, and from, our family above all else, particularly the dedication and determination with which our children pursue even the most minor or menial of tasks around this place. (This is also why we changed the name of the company from Allan Scott Wines to Allan Scott Family Winemakers.) Sure, sometimes we engage in silly experiments, such as a barrel of port we once tried to make (it tasted dreadful), a hybrid wine–beer Josh created not long ago using Sauvignon Blanc grapes and Nelson hops (which we sell on-tap in our restaurant), or even the still we built to try to learn to produce whisky. It's not that we expect any of these things to turn into serious enterprises; it's simply that growing grapes and making wine is quite boring more often than not. Without a little dose of professional entertainment or excitement now and again, our judgment may become clouded or we might start to forget what's most important, which is keeping our family together.

Drinking a toast to my good friend and colleague Daniel Le Brun

This bond, after all, is what allows us to make the sort of wine that brings the same like-minded sort of people back to our front door over and over again.

Cathy and I saw to it that our kids could have done anything with their lives and careers, but all three of them — Victoria, Josh and Sara — have decided to stay local, remain a part of the business and raise families of their own in Marlborough. None of them was gifted a job; each worked hard to find roles for themselves that best fitted their distinct personalities and skills, even though there were difficult times when positions didn't exist for any of them. And yet they kept contributing anyway. They did so, I believe, because Cathy and I opted never to treat our children as children, but as equals. Even when the kids were young, at our family meetings about the business each person's voice has always mattered as much as anybody else's.

I don't know that this was a conscious choice on our part, but I do remember my parents and their parents *acting* old. Everyone, therefore, treated them as old. I always felt that, no matter how many children or grandchildren (seven, at the time of this book's publication) we were to have, I would make an effort to feel only as old as the youngest member of our family, and never talk down to anyone. No matter the circumstance or how much trouble Vic, Josh and Sara ever got themselves into (which wasn't much, as Cathy and I never received one of those dreaded late-night calls from a housemaster or headmaster at school, never mind the police), we did our best to support them as they carved their own paths, which proved ultimately circular.

Like many modern Kiwis, all three kids did an OE. I was most surprised that Vic chose to go to London, as she had hated being away from home when she first went off to boarding school — and I hated her being away. She was our only child then, and for quite some time we thought we may only ever have one. There are seven years between Vic and Josh, not for a lack of trying, but it simply didn't happen in all that time. What did happen, though, was that Vic and I became joined at the hip.

Especially when Cathy worked at night to supplement our income, I was in charge of the house after school and through the evening hours. Vic and I went everywhere together — shopping, out to eat, errands. We would even go into town together on Friday nights. We were inseparable, even during her early teens, when kids tend to want to have nothing to do with their parents. When the day came for her to leave for boarding school in Christchurch, when she was thirteen, I cried and cried and cried — I just sat in the garage and bloody cried as if I were losing my only friend. It took me a long time to realise it, especially considering how unhappy she was her first few years away, but Vic and I got on so well because she was uniquely bright and mature. Part of the reason she was so unhappy away from home wasn't that she missed me or Cathy or Marlborough, but because she was already an adult, and was suddenly surrounded by children day and night.

After school, she returned to Christchurch and entered the management-training programme at the Park Royal Hotel, then moved on to a supervisory

Victoria and Cathy enjoying a glass of our Cecilia bubbles

role at one of the hotel restaurants. She then went to London on her OE and worked for our UK-based wine distributor, where she absolutely thrived. While working in the retail portion of their operation, she handled visiting winemakers as they did their trade visits and dinners in and around London. She ushered along everyone from Napa's Dan and Margaret Duckhorn to well-known Bordeaux producers and *negoçiants* — London has long been the global hub of the Bordeaux wine trade. No ego or reputation was too big to wrangle. Today Vic heads marketing for Allan Scott, and she is an absolute natural, whether she is running a small, local event or handling our larger-scale commitments and sponsorships at home and abroad.

Josh, we knew right away, would grow up to be a different animal altogether — one that constantly surprises us even to this day. Those who know him well are quick to point out that there was never really a question that he would be a winemaker or brewmaster; today, his business card shows his title as 'Serial Fermenter'. In fact, he used to make beer in his dorm room at Christ's College school in Christchurch — something I wasn't even aware of until he mentioned it one night to the assembled guests at a wine dinner over which he and I were presiding.

'Josh, I never knew you did that,' I said. 'I just can't believe you got away with that.'

'Dad,' Josh said, without hesitation, 'I had plenty of customers.'

This is but one example of how there has always been so much more to Josh than meets the eye, and just how clever and calculating he can be. I sometimes worry that he moves through work and life at too fast a pace, and yet he knows when and how to stop and slow down for the purpose of satisfying his curiosity. Josh is always eager to expand his knowledge of the world around him.

Father and son

It was difficult to see, at first, and it was an element of his character that was rather unfortunately suppressed during his years at boarding school, where he didn't exactly shine.

Josh didn't have any particularly strong feelings about being at boarding school, one way or another. By his own admission he really only passed his exams at school through peer pressure, since each study group's percentages were based in part on the success of everyone in the group. (Read: you

We were honoured when Sir Edmund and Lady Hillary visited our winery in 2002, along with Paul Millen, founder of the Marlborough First Light Foundation, a youth charity of which we were a major sponsor.

copped a lot of flak from your classmates if you fell behind.) But there was no thrill in being away from home and on his own, nor a sadness about it, either. School was just something he felt he had to grin and bear, and navigate as best he could; Josh is one of those rare, intelligent creatures who is ever so perfectly ill-suited to the confines of the square, structured classroom environment, such that his intellect wasn't at all apparent even to the most interested and invested of teachers. The shame of it is twofold, in that his unique brand of curiosity and thirst for knowledge was never slaked at school, and also he wasn't able to afford the time to focus on one of his true passions, rugby.

If Josh had stayed in Marlborough and concentrated on rugby, I am convinced he could have made the All Blacks one day, or at least the highest ranks of provincial rugby. With proper training at the right age, he would have been a similar player to Richie McCaw, in that he could get the ball, he was fearless and he never gave up. Especially with the right enforcer either side of him, his physicality and his mindset were perfectly suited to the flanker role. While he never rose to the echelons of professional rugby, I will never forget the joy and excitement he felt when he was selected for the Marlborough Red Devils in his mid-twenties. By that point in his life the possibility of a rugby career was long gone, even with this recognition of his talent, yet what is truly impressive about Josh is that he has no regrets whatsoever about marginalising the sport he loves. (He has been able to dedicate some of his spare time in recent years to multi-sport racing, though, and has clocked multiple competitive finishes in the Speight's Coast to Coast.) Josh makes decisions small and large without ever looking back, his primary motivations being to expand his worldview and never, ever find himself bored.

This is an aspect of his personality I was barely aware existed until he was about twenty and had just finished a winemaking diploma at Nelson Marlborough Institute of Technology. He told me and Cathy that he was applying for a position in Sancerre, France, to work for both Domaine Henri Bourgeois as well as under esteemed vintner Alphonse Mellot at Domaine de la Moussière. Surprisingly, the wineries were seeking staffers who could work in the cellar by day and play rugby at night and on the weekends. Josh and his good mate Scott Berry, from Waipara Downs in Canterbury, both submitted applications for the one position, and both were extended offers. I suppose two Kiwi rugby-playing winemakers are better than one. (Henri Bourgeois never contacted me before they set up Clos Henri in Marlborough, and I often joke with Josh that it's purely because of his time in France, which scared them away from us.)

In all, Josh was away for just shy of four years. He came back home to visit occasionally, but he seemed more and more French each time he returned. We went over to see him as well, and in the small town of Sancerre we were amazed to see he was right at home. He spoke the language, he lived according to local schedules and customs — everything you wouldn't expect a young Kiwi, far away from home, to do. The locals had warmed to him as much as he had to them — although Kiwis will be Kiwis, I suppose.

Cathy and Josh, Burgundy, 2001

More than a decade after Josh's French adventures, I was at a tasting in Santa Fe, New Mexico, when a winemaker standing at a nearby table came up to me and asked in a Gallic accent, 'Are you Josh's father?' I told him that I was, and I asked if he was in Sancerre at the same time as Josh and Scott Berry. 'No,' he said, 'but those two boys … The town is still talking about them.' I told him that perhaps it was best he not relay any particular information or anecdotes. 'I don't think you should check the family silver or anything,' he said, 'but they certainly made an impression!'

The impression left on me, though, was that Josh learned a sense of self-reliance he might not have developed otherwise. Perhaps even more valuable was that he learned various aspects and nuances of growing and vinifying Sauvignon Blanc that almost no one else in New Zealand had at that time.

It all had to do with the subtleties of the grape. While almost everyone else in Marlborough — including us — was trying to make big fruit bombs with lots of acidity that tasted like ripe grapefruit, Josh was learning how you could broaden the flavours and characters, and make a more appealing, integrated Sauvignon Blanc. Most of all, though, he learned the sort of patience with grape-growing and winemaking that Kiwis had yet to identify or practise at the time. Josh also worked a vintage in Napa at Saintsbury, then went back to France to work at Domaine Masson-Blondelet in Pouilly Fumé. While he was there, Josh made several visits to chat with, and learn from, Didier Dagueneau, maker of what many regard as the best Sauvignon Blanc in the world. He also did a stint at Domaine de Terrac in Corbières, in the Languedoc-Roussillon region of southern France.

Josh returned to New Zealand toward the end of 2001 — with a French girlfriend having chased him all the way back. Josh wasn't particularly interested, but his only course of action was to avoid her until she became frustrated and returned home ... which, of course, meant that I was stuck carting her around Marlborough for a couple weeks. It wouldn't have been my recommended method of breakup, but there are certain things that fathers just have to do for their children every now and again — even if that means everybody in town giving me a hard time about Josh having brought back a girlfriend for his dad.

From that time to now, Josh has had an on-and-off role in the winemaking at Allan Scott, but all the while has managed to consult or work in tandem with the winemakers we have had running the cellar. His longest stint away was to launch and run Moa Brewing, which he started as a side project in 2003, producing a simple lager using the same techniques he had learned in crafting sparkling wine. It was an experiment at first, but Moa's unique flavour profile and style caught on quickly. In no time it was in the Blenheim grocery stores, and soon after that in pubs and restaurants up and down New Zealand. After just a couple of years, Josh not only won awards in several competitions but was also able to scale up production, build a brewery behind our house and expand to a wheat lager and a dark lager.

Regrettably, our bank at the time saw no future in the craft beer industry, so we were basically funding and operating the brewery through our winery facilities. Things went from difficult to worse in 2008, when Marlborough experienced a record grape harvest at the same time as the global financial meltdown, slowing exports to a crawl. To his credit, Josh sought a new business partner; he'd heard a rumour that Geoff

Josh with Moa beer — and merchandise

Ross, the former owner of spirits brand 42 Below, was interested in craft beer prospects. Through his venture capital group The Business Bakery, Ross took a majority shareholding along with private equity group Pioneer Capital. The range of beers was expanded, production was ramped up, the brand was modernised and, years on, Moa is the country's largest New Zealand–owned and publicly listed brewery. Josh also became a certified *cicerone* (the official, internationally recognised qualification for beer experts), one of the first in Australasia.

As much as he loved brewing, however, Josh didn't enjoy the marketing pressures that came with the job, mostly because they required that he spend most of his time in Auckland rather than at the brewery making beer. He therefore handed over the managerial reins at Moa and returned home to head our winemaking again, although he can walk across the road from the winery to the brewery to lend a hand whenever he is needed.

When I think back over the past decade or so, none of our wines disappoint, but some are unquestionably better than others — and it is the vintages that Josh has managed outright, or in which he has played even a small, supporting role, that show our wines at their best and truest to our house style. Whether it is a picking decision, having worked the crusher or racking the tank himself, or so tiny a contribution as deciding that a small portion of the blend should be added or removed before bottling, it is his thumbprint that makes most of the difference. I hate to tell him this lest I boost his ego a little too much, but there is no question that when Josh is involved, we make better wine.

Unlike Vic, who loathed boarding school, or Josh, who could take it or leave it, Sara absolutely loved every minute of the experience, and thrived completely in the atmosphere. She had a fantastic life at school in Christchurch, starring in any number of sports teams (especially hockey), and she excelled in the collaborative, camaraderie-driven academic environment. All of her best friends today — even with two kids of her own and years after leaving school — are those from relationships

Sara in 2014

she forged at school. Every time she drives down to Christchurch for a visit, she practically has to pry herself away.

We actually had no idea whether Sara would go away to school excited or in a fury of kicking and hollering, because she and Josh were so close as children. Only a year apart, they always looked after each other in every possible way. I remember when Josh was eight and Sara seven, he would make her lunches for her before school. They would exercise together in the afternoons, and hit the town together on Friday nights from the instant they were able to go out on their own.

Sometimes Josh and Sara would accompany me to wine dinners, even though they were not yet old enough to drink. They attended enough of them — and spent as many hours in the vineyards and winery as anyone — that they knew the script cold. They could talk about our wines perhaps even better than I could. I will never forget one dinner at which they were answering all sorts of questions, some incredibly technical, when a guest asked: 'How old are the two of you?'

Josh and Sara looked at each other, smiled, and Josh responded, 'How old do you want us to be?'

Much like Josh, Sara has a love of sport and is a gifted athlete — especially at hockey. Her Rangi Ruru Girls' School team was one of the best in the country, fuelled in part by her reputation as an uncompromising, hard defender of the ball. She continued to play after school at the club and provincial levels, and it wasn't only this proud father's opinion that she was unlucky not to be selected for the Black Sticks, having represented the Canterbury, Otago and Wellington sides as she moved around the country. She still plays competitively when she can.

One thing Sara particularly excelled at, in ways her siblings never did, was academic study. She never really knew what she wanted to do after finishing school, though, so at first she started out on the track to becoming a lawyer. However, she quickly saw that wasn't right for her, and thought about doing some sort of commerce degree. While she struggled to settle on a career decision, she would work in and around our winery, as well as at other wineries. She did a stint at Spy Valley, and, while she loved working in their cellar, time was closing in on her opportunity to do an OE. Just as Vic had, Sara opted to spend some time on the customer-facing side of the wine business. She lived in London for two years, spending much of the time working at the Harrods wine shop, which mostly inspired her to come back home and complete a diploma in viticulture.

Sara splits her attention between the rows of vines and her two small children. Before Sara started her family, she presided over the most important

Grandchildren Jemima and Ollie Pavey making good use of our boxes

transition our company has seen, which was to develop and implement a plan to shift as many of our vineyards as possible to organic farming practices. It is not something that we boast about, though, as there are plenty of wineries that make shit wine with organically grown grapes. What Sara did was identify the specific blocks on which we could make the fastest and most radical improvements in quality (some of it through organic farming, some of it not), then design the processes through which we could make the transitions.

While it is true that we have made our best wines with Josh in the cellar, we have made even better ones with him running the winery and Sara in charge of the vines. Together, they are formidable, and something special comes through in the wine that subconsciously conveys to everyone who drinks it that the wine is family-made, not factory-made.

Cathy and I shouldn't be at all surprised that our kids turned out the way that they have: Vic has Cathy's intuition; Josh has the same curiosity and intelligence of my mother, which led him to embrace fermentation at a time when Cathy and I were just barely learning it for ourselves; and Sara possesses a natural tendency towards the vineyards, where I eventually found my calling. With each month and year that they expand their respective roles in the business, I am amazed at how much I learn from Vic, Josh and Sara — and how little I have left to teach them.

Of course, Vic, Josh and Sara would also be the first to point out that, even though I claim to be handing off more of the business to them nowadays, I am still as involved as ever. I still do the travelling, the deal-making, the tastings and the dinners, whether they are in Blenheim or Brixton. As much as I hate to admit it to myself (or anyone else), I probably never will let go or step back entirely. Although somehow I suspect that if one day you open a bottle of our wine and it is the best it has ever tasted, that will tell you one thing for certain: Vic, Josh and Sara are now fully in charge, running the show on their own.

I DIGRESS ...

For all the things that make Cathy and I different (and eminently compatible as a result), the one thing we both love is well-designed cars. We are not petrol heads, but we love the lines, the curves, the handling, the feel and the sound of a perfectly engineered vehicle. The funny thing is, neither of us knows the first thing about cars — we just steer them. Yet we have a particular fondness for BMW, so we provide Allan Scott wines to some of the dealerships around New Zealand for their customer-loyalty events. In turn, we upgrade our cars with them every few years.

My true weak spot, however, is Aston Martin. When I was a kid in school, and all the other boys were ignoring the teacher and drawing boats or planes, I would draw cars. The Aston Martin has always been the machine I aspired to own, the one I have gazed at most longingly in glossy car magazines. I never expected that I would get the chance to own one ... or that I would hate it so much.

In early 2007 or so, we took a break from BMW and purchased an Audi, which operates out of the same Christchurch showroom as Porsche. A few months later I received in the mail an invitation to a Porsche day at

263

a racetrack near Christchurch — which I couldn't possibly pass up. And it was absolutely fantastic.

Each guest was paired with a test driver or specialist visiting from the Porsche headquarters in Germany. My instructor was an expert in braking, but he taught me so much more about driving than I ever knew possible. Loop after loop I learned something new as I flew up to and over 240 kilometres per hour. With each pass I learned how to handle the car better. I even mastered the use of the traction control as I navigated a perfect slalom at high speed through a set of cones (though a German yelling at you the entire time makes anyone a quick learner). I left there thinking that I would one day love to own a Porsche.

Of course, they are well aware that this is the effect the driving school will have on all of their guests, so it was only a few days before I was invited back to the showroom for a test drive. I am sure that a German engineer had implanted me with a special tracking and monitoring device that alerted the dealership just as my adrenaline levels were starting to return to normal. *Beep! Time to ring Allan Scott! He's coming off his motoring high!*

I did the test drive, and, as we pulled back into the lot, there it was: a 2004 Aston Martin Vantage. I haven't told anyone until now, but I had already put my name on the list for the new Vantage coming out, and had even paid a $5,000 deposit. Cathy would have killed me if she had known, but I figured that since there was a nine-month wait, maybe my interest would wane by the time the car arrived in New Zealand and I could turn around and sell it for a profit. I would have had to, actually, because I really couldn't have afforded to buy it in the first place. (Although I might have found a way, as I really did love the seat colour I had chosen.)

Anyway, as we climbed out of the Porsche, I sheepishly asked the salesman, 'May I give that Aston a drive?'

'Sure!' he said, and went inside to grab the keys.

I fell in love with it instantly. The car absolutely roared to life — and you could feel the hairs on the back of your neck stand up and salute as you put your foot down on the accelerator. I knew Cathy would be livid with me the instant I came home with it, but I didn't care. I bought myself the toy I had always dreamed of, and got back my deposit on the new model I had on reserve.

As much as I loved tooling around in the car, it got me into plenty of trouble. One time I was driving a friend around Blenheim, and I was pulled over by the police for doing 60 kilometres per hour in a 50-kilometre-per-hour zone. I said to my friend, 'I bet I'm going to get a text any minute.' Instantly, my phone beeped with a message from my daughter Vic: 'I saw that!'

Now, when an iconic supercar such as an Aston Martin passes you on the road, it is natural to think to yourself that it is a ridiculous purchase. Trust me, driving one is even more so. For starters, the car is so low to the ground that you feel like Mr Sulu has sent you to warp-speed even when you are only driving about 60 kilometres per hour (so just imagine what it's like at 160 kilometres per hour). And if you pass a truck, you are about eye-level with the wheel nuts, so you have no visibility whatsoever — it is actually a bit terrifying, which I suppose adds to the thrill a bit. There was one major problem with the car, however: I didn't have nearly enough time to drive it.

Cars are made to be driven — especially Aston Martins. If you don't take them out often enough, the electronics go into sleep mode. They draw down power and eventually don't function properly at all. I can't say for sure, but it is possible that it had been a Friday car, which might be why I was the third owner in just two years. (The first sold it for a profit, while the second bought it after a divorce, and was forced to find a new owner — me — when he and his wife reconciled.)

For a couple of years I oscillated between enjoying brief thrill rides to pulling my hair out over how much money yet another look at the electronics or the gearbox was going to cost me. Eventually, I realised that I couldn't keep pouring money into the car, but also that dreaming of driving an Aston Martin is in some ways more fun than actually owning one, which could even be disappointing considering how often it would just go to sleep, like a lion after a vicious kill. As much as I hated to admit it to myself, I couldn't afford to keep the car, I was too busy to drive it, and for a guy like me, who owns and operates a winery, it was completely useless. I even felt a bit like a tosser in it. So I sold the car to its fourth owner in need of midlife excitement.

I went back to basics: the same useful, straightforward, practical diesel pickup truck I have been driving for years. Although I suppose the Aston did teach me one thing that few other sports-car owners realise, which is that there isn't anything missing from my life. Everything has worked out perfectly.

EPILOGUE

SOME MIGHT ARGUE THAT OUR HOUSE IS WHERE
we made our mark on Marlborough, but sometimes it feels as much like the house is where Marlborough made its mark on us. I think about this often when I drive my truck around the region today, and each time I am amazed that our house and the Allan Scott winery remain where they are, everything still going strong as a family business — mostly because there are hardly any family wineries here anymore. Off the top of my head, I can't name more than half a dozen standalone, brick-and-mortar family-owned wineries in Marlborough. Nearly all of them, regardless of whether they started out as family operations, are now owned by multinational corporations. This isn't a bad thing, per se, in that this makes it possible for epicureans around the world to discover and enjoy Marlborough wine without spending an excessive amount of money. On the downside, it puts tremendous pressure on wineries such as ours, making it remarkably difficult for us to compete and, in turn, survive. It gets more challenging each and every year, as grape prices rise and wine prices on the store shelf fall.

ABOVE: The exterior of our restaurant, with the outdoor area at left
and the upstairs private dining room at right
FACING PAGE: Inside the restaurant, with the cellar-door area at the rear

Fortunately, our few decades' worth of hard knocks have allowed us to be much more smart and strategic today than we were in the past. After the Appellation and Mount Riley partnerships imploded, we vowed we would never get into another, similar situation — and many, many proposals come our way every year, some serious, some less so. We eventually did join a multifaceted partnership in 2004 on a vineyard in Central Otago, after I had been contacted by a manager of equity funds held by a group of relatively high-profile Auckland- and Wellington-based investors eager to buy a vineyard. Wary of the past, I was able to structure the arrangement such that the group bought 75 per cent and we took 25 per cent of a small property, within walking distance of Cromwell. After all of the investors flew down to Queenstown, then spent a couple of days picking grapes on the first harvest, they all fell in love with the place — and instantly wanted to buy more vineyards. I knew, of course, that if a group of investors from outside the wine industry all started purchasing vineyards together, it would

Pinot Noir vines at the Scott Base vineyard, Cromwell, Central Otago

take about five minutes before they would all hate each other, so I sold our 25 per cent share back to them on the condition that I had first right of refusal if they ever wanted out. Sure enough, they purchased more land and all started to go to war with each other, and they wanted nothing to do with the wine business by their second year. We were then able to take over the original vineyard, now the source for our Scott Base label, under which we make a Central Otago Pinot Noir, a Chardonnay and a *méthode traditionelle* sparkling wine.

My point, of course, is that we have to go it alone in order to survive as a family and as a business; and when and where we do forge alliances, we have to anticipate the half-dozen or so escape routes ahead of time. Being passionate about producing high-quality wine, even as we are after

all these years, only counts for so much. It is our dedication to each other, as a family, that fuels our ambition — not to produce larger volumes of wine or trophy-winning wines, but to remain inventive and creative in ways small and large. (We even tried making a Green-hopped Gooseberry Bomb Sauvignon Blanc, basically a wine accented with Nelson Sauvin hops that tastes, well, interesting.)

By keeping our brains engaged and our sense of humour sharp, we manage to suppress any instinct we might have to play things safe and thereby ending up in the position of so many other wineries in Marlborough: as one cog in a multinational corporate machine, making the same wines year after year. As far as we know or believe, the Allan Scott Family Winemakers brand is at its best and most genuine when there is a freethinking, somewhat experimental, slightly quirky family behind it.

One thing we have not done so well, however, over the years, is to step back and let other like-minded families who enjoy our wines get a true taste of what it is like to live and breathe Marlborough, as we have for so long. Only recently has a certain thought begun to resonate: David Hohnen's question to me, in 1983 as he was setting up Cloudy Bay, 'Who wants to live in a vineyard, next to a winery, anyway?'

Certainly not our own children. Vic and her family live in town in Blenheim, as do Josh and his family. Even though Vic and Josh both work at the winery every day, and usually drop by even when they are off the clock, neither looks forward to a day when they can move their families into our house, across the road from the winery. Sara and her husband and children are content to stay in the home they have recently built in a cluster of new houses on the Delta, not far from Renwick. As close as we all are and intend to remain, living on the grounds of the winery isn't a necessity for this any longer. And, frankly, Cathy and I would like to be able to walk out our front door and grab a bite to eat in town now and again with relatively little advance planning or hassle.

To keep the Allan Scott experience fresh and, as a result, the wines tasting their best, it is essential that we all remain excited to come to work each day. Our kids figured this out long before we did. So, in the not-too-distant future, we hope to follow their lead and downsize in town. A little distance, we are certain, can only help with keeping our family focused and engaged. When we do that, we plan to convert our house into a lodge that is open and accessible to the people who have loved and supported us, and enjoyed our wines for so many years.

Want to know what it's like to wake up in the middle of a vineyard each morning? You'll soon be able to. Opening our front door to let the people who enjoy our wine the most stay under the roof where we made our lives and careers, for however long they wish, will only inspire us that much more to maintain and enhance the work that's drawn so many people to us in the first place. We look forward to welcoming you into our home.

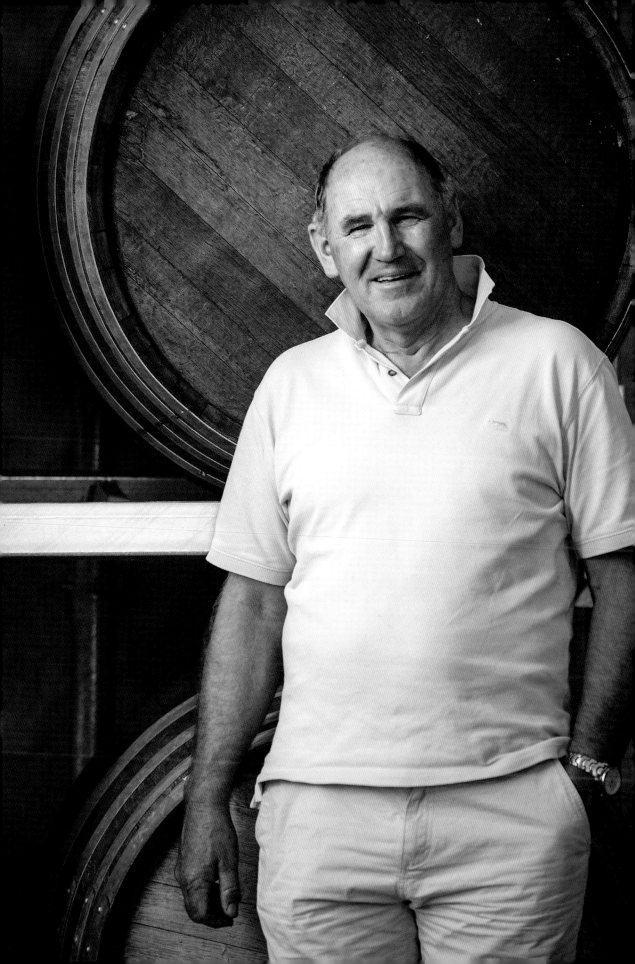

ACKNOWLEDGMENTS

When I initially decided to write a book, I had hoped to dedicate as much of the text as possible to the unsung heroes of Marlborough wine — the planters, the office workers, the tractor drivers and everyone who simply wanted to put in a solid day's work to support their families. To me, their contributions matter so much more to the success of our industry and our region than anyone with deep pockets and the wildest of dreams. Though, in fairness, the relationship is symbiotic.

That's why I must thank everyone at Montana, from the founders to the foremen to the first workers at Brancott. Without you, New Zealand wine would not enjoy the global respect it has today. Equal thanks to everyone at Corbans, who similarly helped blaze New Zealand's wine trail.

Yet I still maintain that the New Zealand wine story would have ended years ago if not for the contributions of Jim Hamilton, Dick Simpson and Clive Drummond. Thanks to all three of you, as well as to Tessa Nicholson. Her thorough interviews with these Marlborough-wine founding fathers

276

proved essential to the creation of this book. Thanks also to *The Marlborough Express*, for additional support with the book's photography.

Thanks to everyone at HarperCollins, particularly Finlay MacDonald, Scott Forbes and Sandra Noakes. You saw and understood this story's potential long before even I did, despite my having lived it. Your vision and support have been extraordinary. Thanks also to photographers Patrick Reynolds, Jessica Jones, Jim Tannock and Tim Hawkins, as well as designer Anna Egan-Reid, a team who made everyone and everything in this book appear so much better-looking than they actually are!

Most of all, thanks to Cathy, Vic, Josh and Sara, who continue to inspire, delight, surprise and impress me every day.

Lastly, my utmost gratitude to everyone, everywhere, who has enjoyed even so little as a sip of Marlborough wine. Your enthusiasm for our labours makes it all worthwhile.

INDEX

Page numbers in *italic type* refer to illustrations.

*HarperCollins*Publishers

First published in 2016
by HarperCollins*Publishers* (New Zealand) Limited
Unit D1, 63 Apollo Drive, Rosedale, Auckland 0632, New Zealand
harpercollins.co.nz

*HarperCollins*Publishers
Unit D1, 63 Apollo Drive, Rosedale, Auckland 0632, New Zealand
Level 13, 201 Elizabeth Street, Sydney NSW 2000
A 53, Sector 57, Noida, UP, India
1 London Bridge Street, London, SE1 9GF, United Kingdom
2 Bloor Street East, 20th floor, Toronto, Ontario M4W 1A8, Canada
195 Broadway, New York NY 10007, USA

National Library of New Zealand cataloguing-in-publication data:

Scott, Allan, 1947-
Marlborough man : a quintessentially Kiwi story of an accidental
wine-industry trailblazer / Allan Scott with Eric Arnold.
ISBN 978-1-77554-057-1
1. Scott, Allan, 1947-. 2. Vintners—New Zealand—Marlborough—
Biography. 3. Wine and wine-making—New Zealand—Marlborough.
I. Arnold, Eric, 1975-. II. Title.
663.20092—dc 23

Cover images © Patrick Reynolds
Cover and internal design by Anna Egan-Reid
Internal photographs by Patrick Reynolds: pages 2–3, 4, 8–9, 10, 13, 14–15, 16, 18, 21, 23, 24–25,
26, 44–45, 46, 62–63, 64, 75, 80–81, 82, 106–107, 108, 128–129, 130, 133, 144, 168–169, 170, 198, 213,
214–215, 216, 246, 248, 250, 258, 270, 271, 278–279; Jessica Jones: pages 6, 22, 196–197, 244–245,
249, 259, 268, 275; Tim Hawkins: pages 266–267, 272–273; Jim Tannock: pages 252, 253, 261;
Fairfax Media NZ / *Marlborough Express*: pages 95, 96, 98, 99, 100, 110, 111, 112, 113, 114.
All other images are from Allan Scott's private archive.

Colour reproduction by Graphic Print Group, Adelaide
Printed and bound in China by RR Donnelley